The Wayward Girls of Samarcand

a true story of the American South

Melton McLaurin & Anne Russell

Bradley Creek Press

Wilmington, North Carolina

Copyright 2012 by Anne Russell & Melton McLaurin

ISBN 978-0-615-63724-2

Cover design by Cissy Russell

Printed by Lightning Source Inc.

With gratitude to BAH, who waked in the middle of the night hearing a voice whisper, "Samarcand."

To Establish a Home for Fallen Women*

Public Law of North Carolina, Chapter 264, 1917

*The name of the State Reform School for Girls has variously
been spelled Samarkand and Samarcand, depending on the era.

Contents

Illustrations

The characters and events in this narrative closely adhere to the historical record. The thoughts and conversations of the characters also are based upon, and sometimes drawn from, that same body of evidence.

1

The Fires

The Superintendent

At just before five o'clock on the afternoon of March 12,1931, Agnes MacNaughton pulled on a long blue Scottish-plaid wool coat, buttoned it up to her chin, and walked out of the Samarcand administration building to her car. The pale sun was setting as a sharp wind made an unusually-cold early March evening seem even colder.

She crossed the yard to her 1929 Ford sedan, a big, black box of an automobile which more and more had become her refuge over the past few months, a momentary escape from the increasingly-impossible responsibilities of running Samarcand Manor Reform School for Girls. Agnes opened the car door and slid behind the wheel, pulled the door shut, adjusted the collar of her coat to warm her neck, and placed her purse on the seat beside her. She did not crank the car, since she had no intention of driving anywhere, had no place to go, really, and had just returned from a three-week vacation insisted upon by friends and staff members. For better or worse, during the past thirteen years Samarcand had been her entire world, her life, and she had devoted herself to it. She believed in the concepts upon which it was founded, felt she could help reclaim damaged lives, and had tried her best to bring this to fruition.

Agnes reached for her purse and fetched a small flask with a hammered silver finish, unscrewed the cap, and sipped from its mouth. She felt the whiskey slide down her throat, its warmth gradually radiating through her body to produce a brief, involuntary shudder. Over the past two years the flask had become a more frequent companion, and its contents, supplied by friends in Raleigh for whom Prohibition posed less difficulty, were her source of solace. She took a second sip, less to ward off the cold creeping into the car than to push back the doubts which over the years had eroded her beliefs and shaken her confidence. The Carolina cold was nothing compared to the cold of her native Scotland, or the bitter cold of Canada, where she had spent her youth. Yet the girls at Samarcand carped about it, as if they were in danger of freezing, their complaints a minor, if constant, irritant.

Samarcand had become her personal caged treadmill, and no matter how hard she ran, things got worse. The trickle of inmates had become a flood of hundreds of society's castoffs, a torrent of girls from broken homes and no homes, from grinding poverty, unwanted, sexually abused, labeled promiscuous, diseased, with diminished mental capacity. It was her job to transform this motley crew into nice, socially-acceptable young women, provide them with an education, teach them to clean and cook and sew, grow and can vegetables, do all necessary which would retool them for a return to the bottom rungs of society's socioeconomic ladder. It was also her task to save their souls, by, as the State required, "teaching the principles of the Holy Bible," a task she took seriously.

Once in what seemed another lifetime, Agnes had hoped for marriage and children, at least one daughter. But life had not played out that way, and instead she had tried, for thirteen

2

years she had tried, to take care of other people's children, begging the legislature for money, struggling to hire female teaching staff for service in an isolated locale, employ nurses and other workers to supervise the operations of a farm and dairy herd.

At first she had stilled her doubts by burying herself in work. Then the Great Depression made inroads. Money for repairs to buildings, furniture, equipment, supplies and fuel, clothing and bedding, and hundreds of necessary items could not be found, no matter how fully she justified her requests nor how much she pleaded. Not only was she denied, but members of the state's Board of Charities, to which the legislature had given oversight of Samarcand and a variety of other juvenile and mental facilities, continually questioned her judgment and challenged her justifications for requests. While some Board members, including Leonard Tufts, who now owned the nearby resort town of Pinehurst, occasionally sent contributions to cover pet projects, library books, or canoes for the lake, such gestures, for which she always expressed deep gratitude, did nothing to meet the basic costs of operation. On occasion she dug into her own pockets to meet the school's expenses. Now more than ever, as families were ripped apart by the Depression, girls kept arriving, defying the rules, testing her authority, until she found herself incapable of suppressing her doubts, yet unwilling or unable to abandon the hopes she had once held for Samarcand.

Agnes peered into the twilight dimness, staring at nothing. It wasn't just the girls. There were so few members of the staff she could trust, who shared her vision and dedication to the mission. It hadn't been that way at first. She used to be able to rely on staff to carry out her orders, but now, it seemed, they questioned everything, some even defying her outright. She had been forced to fire dozens in the past two years, and finding replacements was becoming increasingly difficult, even with the Depression putting people out of work. It was as if suddenly no one wanted to work at Samarcand. The sting of the cold creeping into the car was more than she could bear, so she picked up her purse, opened the door, and stepped to the ground. Thank God she had Estelle and Claire to rely on.

The Very Bad Girl

Margaret Pridgen had been at Samarcand for almost two years, most of the time assigned to Chamberlain Hall. They had been hard years. The past few months had been the worst. She hated the required work, the hot summers without access to a beach, the freezing winters which were colder than in Wilmington with its close proximity to the Gulf Stream. And there was the endless list of rules, much more strict than at home, even with her father's adherence to the Church of the First Born's dictates. She hated the beatings when she broke the rules, the way Agnes MacNaughton and her staff seemed to enjoy watching the girls squirm in pain. Why did people like to hurt people? Why did her father send her to a place which was supposed to show her how to behave well, when the people in charge behaved so cruelly? Most of all she hated not knowing when she could go home. Would she be here forever?

Some girls got to go home, but there seemed to be no rule for how this was to be accomplished. Yet tonight she sensed something in the air, a glimmer of hope she might escape from Samarcand. She couldn't wait to tell Margaret Abernethy. She liked this other Margaret, whom the girls called Peg, thought she was one of the best girls. Margaret Abernethy wasn't mean nor a bully, and she could trust her. Like most of the girls, Margaret Abernethy hated Samarcand, and like all the girls in Chamberlain Hall, she hated Agnes MacNaughton. Energized by the feeling that tonight might be the night which offered them freedom, Margaret Pridgen rushed into Margaret Abernethy's room, her face flushed with excitement. "Peg," she said, flopping down beside her, "guess what I heard."

5

"What?" Peg's tone of voice indicated little interest.

"There's going to be a fire tonight in Bickett Hall. They're going to try to burn it down."

Peg jumped up and faced Margaret. "Who said so?"

"Pearl Stiles and Hilda Godley were talking about it."

"What did they say?" Peg was now all ears.

"Just they was going to set Bickett on fire. A welcome home present for that mean Miz Mac. That's what I heard."

"I hope they burn the whole damn place down," Peg giggled. "Only way to get rid of the bed bugs. I was ate up last night." She hiked her skirt to display the most recent crop of bites on her legs.

Margaret pushed up her sleeves to show similar red lesions. "Me too, Peg. Look here. And I'm supposed to get a beating tomorrow. For nothing. I'm to get beat for nothing. You know, if we burned this building down, they'd have to send us home. They'd be a-scared to keep us here. Even if we only tried to burn it, they might send us home, you reckon? If Pearl and Hilda do burn Bickett, we ought to burn Chamberlain. It's a heap worse than Bickett, we get beat over here all the time."

"How we gonna burn down Chamberlain, Margaret?"

"Let's think about it. There'll be lots of girls would help us. Josephine French, I bet. She's been beat lots of times."

"And Edna Clark," said Peg, warming to the idea. "She's been beat at least three times I know."

"Yeah," Margaret agreed. "Most all the girls would help, I'll bet. Leastways if they are as tired as me of being punished, sleeping in the cold, half freezing, eat up with bugs, not never knowing when you are going home, waiting on that old bitch MacNaughton to say you can leave."

"I'll bet Miss Mac don't never sleep in the cold," Peg said, giggling. "Probably sleeps with her dog Jsck. Thinks he's her boyfriend. But maybe not; she's got old lady Stott to keep her warm."

"More like Miz Crenshaw with Miz Mac," Margaret responded. "You know what was her job before she came here?" Peg shook her head no. "Miz Crenshaw was an animal trainer for a circus!" Peg's eyes grew wide. "Elephants! Can't you just see her strutting around with a big stick, whipping on that elephant butt?"

"Maybe Miz Mac's so mean because she's a grownup woman with nobody to keep her warm. I don't want to be like that, do you?" asked Peg. "A crotchety old maid nobody likes. That's what witches are, old maids." She pressed her lips into a thin line. "You notice she never smiles, except when she's watching somebody get beat. Then she puts on a smile like she's found the prize in a Cracker Jack box. Maybe that's why she named her dog Jack, and she don't care if he bites us."

"We burn down Chamberlain, maybe she'll get trampled in the stampede. Then they'll have to send us home. If they burn Bickett, I say let's do it. We'll think of a way. Come on, let's go eat, see what happens."

At a little after half past six, Agnes MacNaughton sat in the dining hall at the superintendent's table, enjoying conversation with her usual three table mates. Estelle Stott, eight years her personal secretary, sat next to her. A tall, thin woman with an angular but pleasant face, she wore her iron-grey

7

hair closely cropped. Across from them sat Claire Crenshaw, a thick, plain woman in her mid-fifties, the campus discipline officer, who, like Agnes and Estelle, resided in the administration building. Next to her was Judy Ross, a petite blonde in her late forties, the youngest of the group and matron of Chamberlain Hall, designated the campus "discipline hall," residence of those girls deemed troublemakers.

"The girls seem excited tonight," Claire observed, "on edge. That's usually not a good sign."

"Oh, I don't think there's a problem. Probably thrilled to see Agnes back on campus," Estelle responded with a trace of irony.

"I doubt the girls are eager to see me, Estelle," Agnes said. "It's good to be back, but I must admit I needed the rest. The Lord knows the pressures of running this place can wear a person down, body and soul. My sister is concerned about me being here so long."

"Unless they give us more money, things are only going to get worse," said Judy.

"I think we all know that's not going to happen any time soon," Agnes replied, thin lips tightening and eyes narrowing. Excited chatter among the girls escalated, interrupting the women's conversation.

The girls began to leave their tables and rush toward the door. "Fire!" one of them shouted. "It's a fire in Bickett Hall."

"Oh, my God!" said Agnes, her worst fears manifesting. Samarcand was a tinder box, a disaster waiting to happen. One good fire and a stiff wind, no telling what would go up in flames. "Claire, you and Judy get these girls under control. Estelle, see

8

if Miss Moore has all the girls out of Bickett. I'll ring down to the barn to see if Joe and Larry are still there, to get the fire hydrants working. Then I'll call the Carthage fire department. And I want everyone ready to do what has to be done, so turn the staff out now."

Within minutes, the two men at the barn responded to Miss Mac's call, and connected the fire hydrants which had been installed two years earlier at the insistence of the insurance company. But when the men opened the hydrants, they proved useless. Water trickled rather than gushed, producing a stream which could only be used to supply water for a desperately-formed bucket brigade of teachers and staff. Haphazard and frantic, their efforts were no match for the fire. Within minutes, smoke curled from an area near the chimney. Flames breached the exterior walls; shooting into the night sky, the orange glow lit the darkness.

A stiff March wind lifted a steady stream of sparks, winking and blinking, and a wall of heat pushed back the cold, making it impossible to approach the burning building. Agnes MacNaughton stood outside, a shawl around her shoulders, momentarily transfixed. The ides of March, she mused, beware the ides of March. Et tu, Brutus! Caesar was assassinated on the ides of March. The ides were three days away, nothing to do with Samarcand. But in Scotland it was already March 13, closer to the ides, and she was born in Scotland. Could there be any significance? Stop it, Agnes, she mentally slapped herself, you're letting your imagination run away with you. Nobody's going to kill you. They don't hate you that much. Please God, she heard herself pray out loud, don't let the sparks ignite another building. All the girls were outside now, ignoring her, watching the blaze, talking, in constant motion. Some were jumping up and down, cheering the flames, others laughing. She glimpsed Claire and Judy moving about the outer edge of the semicircle the girls had formed, facing the front of Bickett, trying without much success to get their attention.

Agnes glanced up once more at the flames and sparks ascending from Bickett into the night, pulled her shawl close around her, and marched to the front of the semicircle of animated adolescent girls, stood in the center, her body silhouetted against the fire's glow. First the cheering stopped, then the laughter, then the talking. The girls fell into silence, eyes fixed on their overseer, who stood motionless, silent, listening to the crackling of the flames.

"Girls," she said, her voice firm, but without shouting, "you must return to your residence halls NOW. I understand your curiosity, but this fire is dangerous, and until it is under control, you have to go inside. The Carthage fire department will soon be here. I don't want any of you getting hurt. Follow your matrons and go back to your rooms in the halls not affected by the fire."

A grumble of disappointment swept through the semicircle as the girls grudgingly obeyed. Within ten minutes they were all inside and Agnes MacNaughton breathed a sigh of relief. By now flames engulfed the rear of the building, and still the Carthage Fire Department had not arrived. She spotted Estelle and Claire searching for stragglers. "Come on, let's head back to the administration building. Nothing we can do now but wait for the fire truck. At least they can dowse the ashes."

Seeing Bickett burn energized Margaret Pridgen so much she could barely stand it. Miss Ross had ordered the girls to go to their rooms in Chamberlain, and for about ten minutes they complied. Then they began to flit from room to room, whispering about Bickett. Margaret sneaked into the hallway, collected Marian Mercer, and ran to Peg's room. "I told you!" she announced. "I told you they were going to burn Bickett, and damn if they didn't. If they can do it, we can do it. Let's exterminate. Burn out the bedbugs! And too bad the whole building goes down with them. They'll have to send us home. I'm not going to miss this chance. If you won't help, I'll burn it myself. I want to see my, umm, baby sister again. She's walking by now."

"I'll help," volunteered Peg. "If you'll tell me what to do."

"Me, too," Marian agreed.

"First, we find some matches," said Margaret. "Then we get some rags, go up in the attic, and set the rags on fire."

"You want to do it now?" asked Peg.

"Not just yet. Let things quiet down. I don't want Miss Ross catching us. Josephine, Virginia, Mary Lee Bronson, you can help. You all hate this place much as I do." After more discussion about how to enter the attic, the three slipped out of Peg's room and began to solicit supplies from girls they trusted not to snitch. As Margaret predicted, they quickly obtained matches and rags, mostly old stockings with holes in them. They retreated back to Peg's room, unobserved by Miss Ross, accompanied by Thelma Council and Ollie Harding, who insisted on helping.

"Now what do we do, Margaret?" asked Peg.

"I know," Marian said. ""Let's go to the kitchen. We can get into the attic there, put a chair on a counter and climb right in.""

11

"That's it," agreed Margaret. "That's what we'll do. Peg, you watch out for Miss Ross. Me and Marian will get in the attic and light the fire. Thelma, you and Ollie make sure none of the girls don't bother us."

Within minutes Margaret and Marian were in the kitchen, Peg stationed at the door as lookout while they climbed into the attic. Thelma and Ollie watched the hallway to intercept any girls who might come out of their rooms and get curious. Margaret pulled herself up first, reached down for the matches and rags Marian held up to her, then helped Marian into the attic. "Over here," Margaret said, stooping to avoid hitting her head on the low timbers. "Let's start it over here, near where the roof meets the floor. That way it should catch quicker."

Minding their heads, Margaret and Marian carefully placed several stockings in a line so they touched both roof and attic floor. "You think they'll burn?" Marian asked.

"Of course they will. They're cotton, ain't they? And they're dry. Give me some matches."

Margaret took the box of wooden safety matches and carefully lit the line of stockings at both ends and in the middle. The girls stepped back and watched the stockings for a few moments, until bright yellow flames licked the roof at all three places, then scurried down their improvised ladder into the kitchen, replaced the chair, and ran down the hall.

"Let's go back to our rooms til someone smells smoke and yells fire," Margaret said. "Then we can all go outside and watch it burn."

She had barely gotten into her room before she heard some girl running down the hall screaming, "Fire, there's a fire in the attic." Damn, thought Margaret, annoyed the fire had not burned longer undetected. She heard Miss Ross in the hall knocking on doors, ordering girls to get out, and Margaret the fire starter left her room to join the other girls outside.

Agnes MacNaughton had just begun to enjoy her coffee with Estelle and Claire when a girl from Chamberlain burst into the Administration Building. "Fire, Miz Mac, there's a fire in Chamberlain, in the attic."

"Claire," Agnes ordered, "go over to the dining hall and see if the men are still there. If they are, send them to Chamberlain. Estelle, come with me." Agnes and Estelle arrived at Chamberlain just moments before the two farm workers. Miss Ross had the girls standing in a group well back from the building, excited and noisy, but under control. Agnes looked for flames but saw none, nor could she see any smoke. She took charge of the girls and sent Miss Ross and the two men into the building to determine whether the fire remained a threat. With a ladder from the locked pantry, the men entered the attic through the kitchen entrance used by the girls, called for a bucket of water, then for a second bucket, and soon retreated down the ladder to announce the conflagration was extinguished. The fire, they said, was obviously set, but oak planking, not heart pine, had been used in that section of the attic. Though badly charred, it had not burst into flames. With Estelle, Agnes began to walk toward the administration building, aware the fires that night had been deliberately set and hoping there would be no more, while Judy Ross herded the girls back inside Chamberlain.

13

A disappointed but determined Margaret Pridgen marched down the hallway and burst into Peg's room and quickly shut the door behind her. "Why you think it didn't catch?" Peg asked.

"I don't know. Maybe the damn socks didn't burn long enough. Maybe we should have lit more of them, in more places."

"Looks like we missed our chance," Peg said. "Ain't no way we're going back in that attic."

"Don't have to," retorted Margaret. "I'll set the damn fire myself this time, in my room, and I know just how to do it. You got any of them paper dress patterns?" The tissue-like pattern paper, Margaret knew, would make perfect kindling, if she could find enough. The girls used it all the time in sewing classes, making jumpers and pinafores, skirts and blouses, aprons and dresses. No reason not to use it to start a fire, burn down Chamberlain. "To start the fire. I've got more in my room. Give me what you have."

Peg rummaged around and produced a dozen faded envelopes, each featuring drawings of the finished items to be constructed using the tissue patterns folded neatly inside. She handed them to Margaret. "You think that's enough?"

"With what I've got, sure. They'll burn quick and catch the clothes in my closet. The whole room should be on fire in no time."

"You gonna burn your own clothes?" Peg asked incredulously, as if the idea of the loss of personal property to a fire had never occurred to her.

"Of course, so long as they work," Margaret replied, gathering up the patterns Peg had found. "Besides, Peg, they'd

14

get burned anyway!" Back in her room, Margaret shut her door and placed a chair in front of it. She collected Peg's envelopes, opened her closet, and pulled all the patterns from their paper packets, crumpling them into fist-sized balls and placing them on the floor beneath her hanging clothes, covering the balls of tissue paper with the packets. She took two thin cotton blouses which hung in the closet and placed them lightly atop the mound of paper. Then she stepped back, pulled a box of matches from her pocket, struck one and lit an end of the mound, struck another and lit the other end. The two tiny sparks flashed through the tissue papers, turning them into a mass of flames which quickly ignited the packets, the two blouses, and leapt to clothes hanging in the closet. Realizing she had succeeded with her task, Margaret smiled with satisfaction and retreated into her room and closed the closet door to insure the fire would continue to grow unnoticed. She watched as smoke crept from beneath the closet door, then flames, and she felt the heat of the fire on her face. She ran from the room, closed the door behind her, and ran down to Peg's room.

"It's happening," she cried, grabbing Peg and jumping up and down in an excited jig. "They won't put this one out."

"Fire!" she heard one of the girls yell, "fire on the hall!" Margaret opened the door and peered toward her room. Smoke was pouring from beneath her door now, snaking into the hall way. Girls ran from their rooms, yelling to others to get out. Margaret saw Judy Ross run from her room, unlock some of the rooms in which girls had been locked for punishment, and throw her keys to Edna Clark, who opened the last punishment doors.

"Come on," Margaret said, seizing Peg's hand, "it's time to save ourselves."

15

Outside, the residents gathered in front of Chamberlain in tightly-packed clusters of six and seven, conversing, oblivious to the cold. Near Margaret's room flames had eaten through to the exterior and begun to climb the outside of the building. Margaret glimpsed a girl running toward the administration building, and noted that girls were beginning to emerge from other residence halls and move toward the burning building. "Stay together, girls," she heard Miss Ross shout. Margaret had no intention of leaving and could not imagine why anyone would. Watching Chamberlain burn was the most exciting thing to happen since she had been brought here.

The Road to Samarcand

As the girls stomped their feet and the fire crackled, Margaret felt a shiver of joy from head to toe, and she remembered the day she was taken to Samarcand, a late morning in June 1929 when she was thirteen. A week earlier her father had taken her to a magistrate to tell her to stop "running around" with boys, and the magistrate had ordered her to this place she never heard of, without saying how long she'd be gone. She didn't consider herself a "bad girl," although she did like boys. She had only messed around with one boy, her cousin Richard, whom she secretly considered her boyfriend. And she would not have done that if Richard hadn't borrowed his brother's car that night. She stayed out late with him, down at the beach, which was only a few miles away, and they messed around in the back seat. It felt good to be alone together, without all her brothers and sisters, away from her parents and the elders of the church. The birth of her baby sister only a few weeks earlier had defined Margaret becoming a grownup instead of a child, for she was the firstborn of this batch of her father's children, the oldest one, who had the responsibility of caring for those younger, and she had a right to do something on her own, the way grownups did, without getting permission. She had a right. Richard thought so, too.

Her father saw things differently. Upset and angry, he knew something had to be done to control his daughter. Margaret blamed their Church of the First Born, the Old

17

Apostolic Lutherans, which they attended every Sunday. It was a very strict church, stricter even than the Baptists, and controlled by the Elders, always old men. They had the power, which they often used, to demand that wayward church members, especially women, stand before the congregation, confess their sins, and beg forgiveness or otherwise be disfellowshipped, shut off from the church and its members. Her father must have told them about Margaret staying out with the boy, for the Elders ordered her to confess. Margaret refused. The public humiliation was simply too great to bear, and no amount of pleading by either the Elders or her father could change her mind. Furious and embarrassed, her father and mother agreed she should go before the magistrate, for they had more than enough children to take care of, and if Margaret wasn't going to behave herself, she would be worse than no use to them.

Margaret didn't know where the state reform school was. She wondered what Sam-ar-cand would be like, and how long she would have to stay. She said the strange word over and over under her breath. What did it mean? Sam-ar-cand. She saw the new, shiny black Ford with silver letters spelling New Hanover County above a golden, five-starred badge, with Sheriff's Department written below. A light, humid breeze stirred the early morning air, bringing with it the odor of salt marsh, as the matron took her from her father and walked her to the car parked at the foot of the court house steps. A deputy sat behind the steering wheel, his left arm resting on the window frame. He knew it would be a long hot ride. The matron, a stout, middle-aged woman stuffed into a brown uniform, walked Margaret to the opposite side of the car, opened the rear door and motioned her inside. Then the matron walked back to the driver's side, opened the door and took her seat behind the driver. She didn't speak. The deputy shifted the car into first, and they set off.

They drove to the foot of Market Street, bumped up a gangway, and onto the ferry. Margaret had seen it many times, slowly negotiating the Cape Fear River's dark waters, its deck filled with automobiles and trucks and passengers. She flinched as its engines surged to life, vibrating the steel decking. Slowly the ferry pulled away from its moorings, great swirls of water kicked up by its propellers. Sitting in the car, windows rolled down, Margaret heard the churning of the water. She watched flocks of black-headed seagulls accompany the ferry, wheeling in the air, hoping someone would throw a tidbit. Within minutes the engines slowed, and the ferry nudged the docks on the other side of the river. The gangway came down with a thump, and the black Ford followed the line of traffic ashore.

Once on the road, the city and marshes disappeared quickly behind them, replaced by the flat emptiness of pine forests on either side, an unrelenting green wall broken by patches of cultivated land. Within an hour the heat enveloped them, creating shimmering mirages on the blacktop surface. Margaret could feel sweat trickling from beneath her arms, running down her body. She watched as the matron fanned herself with a cardboard fan stapled to a flat wooden handle, a picture of a kneeling Jesus praying in the garden printed in bright blues and purples on the fan. Margaret knew from Sunday School that He was in the Garden of Gethsemane, praying He might not die, for God to spare him. She reckoned that since God didn't help Jesus, her own prayers had little chance of being answered. The deputy pushed out the wing vent on his window, and Margaret felt a flow of hot air brush her face. They passed through villages, whistle stops on the Atlantic Coast

19

Line Railroad which ran west from Wilmington into the interior, into Green Swamp, a vast, watery tangle of pines and cypress trees, with every type of climbing vine.

Margaret concentrated on the passing scenery, as swamp and woods gave way to more open spaces of cultivated land. She was riding through one of the state's poorest regions, a patchwork of tobacco and cotton farms on sandy pine barren soil, most tilled by tenants. The tall, broad-leafed plants she saw in the fields she recognized as tobacco. The Church of the First Born allowed tobacco use, for smoking and dipping and a chew. She recognized the two-story wood structures, narrow and windowless curing barns, which stood near the fields, where green tobacco was turned a golden yellow. She knew the golden leaves were used to make the cigarettes she shared with Richard, and she liked the tobacco taste though it was sharp on her tongue, the smoke burned her eyes, and it could make her teeth yellow if she smoked long enough, bring on a cough deep down in her chest. One of her uncles had trouble breathing and spit into a rag because of his smoking. But smoking was kind of fun. Richard had shown her how to blow rings by holding smoke in her mouth and exhaling with her tongue stuck out. Sometimes they had smoke-ring contests, which Richard usually won. Smoking was what let people know you were grown up, although she didn't understand why this is true, perhaps something about fire being dangerous.

Riding in the car, she glimpsed short green plants which were cotton. The bolls were just beginning to form, but in a few weeks they would open, white puffs like clouds, which her father sometimes brought home from when he traveled inland on carpentry jobs. Margaret knew cotton was important to North Carolina, and the mills made cotton cloth for dresses and sheets and curtains and all kinds of things. Important as it was for a crop, the miles and miles of fields bored her, and she wished the car ride would end. She closed her eyes, thought about Richard and the beach, and hoped she wouldn't have to stay very long at Samarcand. She opened her eyes when she heard a log truck rumble onto the highway from a dirt road stretching back into the woods. The load of pine logs looked like giant tooth picks wrapped in huge metal chains, stacked between metal poles on the open trailer. The deputy weaved the sheriff's car to the left, checked for oncoming traffic, and sped past the truck, whipping back into the right lane. She enjoyed the car's rapid acceleration and deceleration which caused the matron to brace her feet and grab hold of the car seat.

After some time, the deputy began to talk with the matron. Margaret tried to ignore them and pretend she was at the beach, but it was impossible to shut out their conversation, so she halfway listened, though she really didn't know nor care what they were saying. Something about a strike by mill workers in a place called Gastonia. The deputy said the strike was caused by a bunch of Commonists trying to destroy America. He said the governor sent in the National Guard to protect the mill owners and their property from the strikers. He was glad the mill owners had thrown the strikers out of the houses owned by the company, it was what they deserved for listening to Commonists and refusing to work. The matron said she understood the need to protect property, but the mill owners throwing workers out in the streets was mean. Margaret wasn't sure what the National Guard was, although it sounded like an army, nor what Commonists were, except they must be for the common people. She silently agreed with the matron it was mean to throw people into the streets. She knew some of the children of workers at the

Delgado textile mill in Wilmington, and they seemed as nice as anybody even though they were poor. The conversation between the matron and deputy always stopped when they reached a town.

Riding through the small towns strung out along the highway was the most exciting part of the trip. Margaret noticed they all seemed alike, lacking the tall buildings and rows of great houses she liked so much in Wilmington, some of which her father had worked on as a carpenter. Each town had railroad tracks running alongside or through the middle of the road, and several times they had to stop as a train rolled slowly by, giving Margaret a chance to try to read where the railway cars came from. Several towns had large, cavernous buildings on their outskirts, which Margaret knew were tobacco markets. She had been inside a tobacco warehouse once, up at Burgaw where her father had a day's work. White men in overalls clustered around bundles of yellow tobacco, and black men moved baskets about the warehouse floor. A row of stores bordered Burgaw's main street, like the small towns they were now passing through on the way to Samarcand. They all had a furniture store, clothing store, drug store, small restaurant, filling station, and sometimes a squat building with an American flag, which was the post office. Margaret liked the dime store, with big gold letters above the door spelling out K R E S S. Some larger towns had courthouses, always on a center square, like in Burgaw. They drove through these towns slowly, only stopping at a red light, and each town was left behind as the deputy accelerated on the open road.

One town was different, where they stopped for a chicken salad sandwich on white bread, and a soda fountain Coke, in a real glass, not a bottle. She had never seen a town so neat, so

22

pretty. The houses were big and beautiful, all freshly painted, with lush green lawns bordered by blooming shrubs and flowers, like in magazines. This town had hotels, each with a grand lawn and garden, cut and trimmed. The shops were fancy, almost like cottages. Margaret had never seen any place like this. At lunch the deputy and the matron said this place was Pinehurst. Margaret ate her sandwich and listened, taking only an occasional sip from her fountain coke, hoping to make it last longer. The deputy said this was a famous golf resort for rich people. A man named James Walker Tufts created Pinehurst, and made millions of dollars selling a soda fountain machine he invented. Margaret heard his name as "Mr. Toughs," which she thought an odd last name for someone so rich, though maybe he was rich because he was tough and wouldn't let anyone take away his money. She could understand why he made so much money, because everybody liked ice cream.

The deputy said Mr. Toughs was sort of a health fanatic and wanted to build a hospital in a warm climate for people with TB. Margaret knew TB was an awful disease, causing people to be sent away for a long time to make them get well. The deputy was saying, "Mr. Toughs came down here about the time I was born, and he bought up a lot of land, which wasn't much good except for growing grass and pine trees, but was plenty cheap. When the hospital idea didn't work so good, he turned his property into a golf resort for wealthy folks from the north like himself, and he spent a fortune fixing the place up. It's not like any other place in North Carolina. My daddy used to work for Mr. Toughs when he was a boy, help keep up the golf course."

Margaret tried to imagine what a fortune would look like. It had to be a lot of money. She knew what golf clubs looked like, because she had seen men at the city golf course in Wilmington using these sticks to hit little white balls over the sand and grass. The deputy said this Mr. Toughs brought some famous man down from New York to design the whole village. The deputy kept talking to the matron, who acted like she was interested. "Mr. Toughs hired a man all the way from Scotland to build the golf courses," he was saying. "Pretty soon trainloads of Yankees showed up to play golf. Even John D. Rockefeller came down to North Carolina." Margaret wondered why John D. Rockefeller, who her daddy said was the richest man in the world, would come to anything in North Carolina. Pinehurst, she thought, must be a very special place, even magical.

The deputy went on talking, even though he was finished eating his lunch, as if he was in no rush to get to where they were headed. He seemed fascinated with Mr. Toughs. "He hired lots of famous people to entertain his guests when they weren't playing golf. Like that shooting woman out West, Annie Oakley." The matron sat up straighter at the mention of a shooting woman. "He paid her a lot of money to come to Pinehurst before the war and she stayed awhile, teaching rich folks how to shoot. She could hit one, two, three, clay pigeons on the fly."

At last the matron and deputy got up to leave. The rest of the trip went quickly. Her escorts were now more talkative, perhaps because they were about to reach their destination. Or perhaps, thought Margaret, because they enjoyed the chicken salad sandwiches and the fountain cokes. Whatever the reason, they chatted in a friendly manner as Margaret gazed out the window. The deputy said Samarcand used to be a boy's school, but a Mr. Pumpelly, he named Samarcand. Margaret stifled a giggle. Pum-pelly, sounded like plump belly, another silly name!

The deputy interrupted Margaret's thoughts to tell her Samarcand was just ahead. He turned left off the highway onto miles of dirt road with ruts and washed-out holes. He kept the car in second gear, sometimes shifting to low, as the car bounced and careened down the road, jostling Margaret so badly she had to hold on tightly to avoid being thrown into the matron, who was balancing herself on the back seat by holding onto the driver's seat in front of her. He kept talking to the matron about Samarcand as the car traveled deeper and deeper into pine forest, away from anything resembling civilization. The deputy said the reform school was like a small town now, with girls coming from all over the state. It had its own farm and a dairy herd.

Suddenly Margaret saw a large white wooden sign with SAMARKAND MANOR in black letters. The dirt road swerved to the right, and the deputy guided the car to the left onto an even narrower lane flanked by rows of crape myrtles, their watermelon pink flowers in full bloom, and magnolias, each with a few enormous white blossoms. The trees gave way to a clearing, and Margaret got her first taste of Samarcand. She thought the deputy was right, the cluster of buildings looked like a small town. At the end of the lane was the most impressive building, a two-story brick structure with giant white columns, one story wings at each side. Left and right of the main building were rows of what appeared to be dormitories, six of them, nondescript two-story frame buildings. A slightly-smaller white frame building had rounded columns, which was the school, near the dorms. Across the lane, in a stand of young pines, was a small church. A playground ended at the edge of a pine forest.

Samarcand was a great deal grander than Margaret had imagined, which excited her. Maybe her father had done the

25

right thing sending her here. She wanted to get back in school, since they took her out of school in Wilmington so she could help at home. She now had hope her stay here would not be the terrible experience she feared, and she would soon be sent home. The car rolled to a stop in front of the main building, the matron got out, came around the car, and opened the door for Margaret. They walked together up the wide wooden stairs, through double doors, into a huge parlor, where a lady dressed in grey sat behind a desk. She directed them to an office on the other side of the room. It had a wooden door with a frosted glass window on which was painted, in crisp, black letters

Agnes B. MacNaughton

Superintendent

When the matron knocked on the door, a voice from inside, firm but not unpleasant, with a slight accent unlike Margaret had ever heard before, instructed them to enter. The matron ushered Margaret into a large room furnished with a plain wooden desk, before which were three straight-back chairs. A small table with two additional chairs sat to the left of the room. The woman behind the desk did not rise, but motioned them into two of the chairs in front of her. As they took their seats, the matron pulled a manila folder from beneath her left arm. Margaret had glimpsed the folder in the car, seen her own name typed on the tab. As the matron handed the superintendent the folder, Margaret noticed something printed in ink, all capital letters, just beneath her name. It said "VERY BAD." Margaret heard the matron say, "Superintendent MacNaughton, this is Margaret Pridgen of Wilmington." Stunned by what she had just read, Margaret barely heard the brief exchange between the superintendent and the matron which followed.

26

"Margaret Pridgen, welcome to Samarcand," she heard the superintendent say. She nodded a response and trained her attention on the woman who spoke, sitting rigidly upright, arms resting on the desktop. She wore a black dress with a white lace collar, her hair, reddish blonde and wavy, not quite covering her ears. Her hazel eyes focused on Margaret, and her lips, straight and thin, did not smile. Hers was an official face, not unfriendly, but impassive. Margaret wondered what Agnes MacNaughton would think of the printed letters under Pridgen on the manila folder, and how what she thought about them would affect Margaret's stay at Samarcand. She had no way to know it, but Agnes MacNaughton of the cool green eyes and impassive face would control her life for the next two years.

Suddenly Margaret heard Peg calling "Margaret! Margaret! Are you alright?" Peg's voice snatched her from her reverie and back into the warmth of the crackling fire and the excited chatter of the other girls.

"Yeah, Peg, I'm fine," she answered. "Couldn't be better. The fire's beautiful, don't you think? And besides," she added, "It smells good."

As Margaret and Peg stood outside watching the flames consume Chamberlain, Agnes MacNaughton sat in her office wondering when the Carthage Fire Department would arrive, hoping the Bickett and Chamberlain fires had not been intentionally set. Suddenly her door flew open and an agitated girl rushed in. "Chamberlain's on fire again!" the girl wailed, "Come quick, Miz Mac!" The announcement set Agnes' mind spinning. Could this be possible? What could she do? What could she tell the Board of Directors about this disaster? Where was the Carthage Fire Department? Mother of God, would there be more fires? Were the girls safe?

She quickly decided on a course of action. "Claire, Estelle, go down to Chamberlain and help Miss Ross keep the girls in line. I'll call CJ."

Sheriff Charles J. McDonald took Agnes MacNaughton's call at home just before eight o'clock in the evening. Known to all as CJ, the sheriff was one of the most respected men in Moore County, and easily the best known. The McDonald family, Highland Scottish immigrants, had resided in Moore County for more than a hundred and fifty years as one of the region's prominent families. After stateside service as a lieutenant in the First World War, CJ returned to Carthage and obtained employment with the County Highway Office, working his way up to superintendent of county highways. When the incumbent sheriff announced he would not seek reelection in 1928, CJ, married with children, entered the race and won the county's most significant elected office. Now in his mid-fifties, he was known for his common-sense approach and was respected for his professional treatment of anyone involved in a case. Over the years he had come to know Agnes MacDonald well, personally as a fellow Scot, and professionally as Samarcand superintendent. He had become accustomed to her occasional calls for help in locating a girl trying to escape from Samarcand, and usually he and his deputies quickly located and returned the offender. It was one of the department's easier tasks; the escapees simply had nowhere to go. He and his deputies could find the escapee along the railroad tracks which ran just north of Samarcand, or beside the highway leading to Carthage to the west, Pinehurst to the east. Infrequently one of the older girls would head south through the forest for the South Carolina state line, no more than twenty-five miles away, and CJ.would be forced to order Deputy Larry Mudd to track her down with blood hounds.

The sheriff didn't particularly like Agnes MacNaughton, but he admired her. He had always considered her competent and well-meaning, and he understood how difficult her task must be, trying to bring order into the chaotic lives of girls whom nobody much wanted, girls who might tempt the soldiers at the military base in nearby Fayetteville, and pass on venereal disease, or worse still, become pregnant with babies who had no homes. The Depression had taken its toll on the budget of the sheriff's department, and CJ knew Samarcand also must be struggling to make ends meet. He had always thought Agnes was too severe in her expectations of the girls, and suspected that tough economic times had not softened her approach. On the phone tonight, however, he heard a different Agnes MacNaughton, agitated, afraid, losing control, her voice filled with desperation. "CJ, you have to get over here right now," she was pleading. "Bickett's almost completely burned down and now Chamberlain is burning. I called the Carthage Fire

Department about Bickett, and they still aren't here. We don't have anything to fight big fires with." Her voice became shrill. "This is arson, CJ, and I'm afraid there will be more. You'll have to arrest some of the girls, keep the others safe. This is arson, arson for sure. You must come immediately."

He tried to soothe her. "Calm down, Miz Mac. I'll be there fast as I can, thirty minutes tops, we'll sort all this out. I'll see what's keeping the Fire Department, light a fire under them, excuse my poor attempt at humor. You keep the girls safe until we arrive." He hung up and called Larry Mudd, his chief deputy. "Larry, we have to go to Samarcand Manor, NOW. Miz Mac just called; she's got two buildings ablaze out there and expects more fires. I'll stop by the courthouse, you pick up the bus and follow me. We may have to transport some prisoners. She's pretty sure some of the girls set the fires, and she's probably right."

Swinging by the fire station, the sheriff spied the town's lone engine ready to pull out, firemen clambering on board. "Had trouble getting her started," one of the men called, before the sheriff could ask any questions. "We'll be there soon." Not bothering to stop, CJ drove to the courthouse, honked his horn at Deputy Mudd to follow him in the bus, and headed for Samarcand.

Five miles from Samarcand, CJ could see the glow from the fires radiate through the night sky. Within two miles, he began to smell pine resin smoke. Turning off the highway onto the dirt road, he drove toward the central campus, into the orange glow which silhouetted the buildings against the surrounding darkness. Smoke hung in the air like fog and the scent of burning pine was almost choking. About a hundred yards on his right he glimpsed what remained of Bickett Hall, smoldering roof timbers scattered about a bed of red-hot ash.

30

Another few yards was what remained of Chamberlain, roof collapsed, parts of two walls still standing, stubbornly refusing to yield to the flames. Girls filled the yard, milling about, watching the fires. As he drew closer, he could hear them yelling to one another. Staff members moved along the perimeter of the girls clustered in several large groups, the staff attempting to keep their charges under control. CJ drove slowly to the administration building, followed by Deputy Mudd in the bus. Stepping from his car, he saw the Carthage Fire Department's sole ancient engine lumbering into the central campus, sirens blaring. "Now that," he called to his deputy, "is a sure case of inadequacy. At least they can water down the ashes, make sure the fires don't spread."

"Yeah," Larry Mudd replied, "ain't this a damn mess?"

Agnes MacNaughton met the officers at the door, holding it open with one hand while waving to them with quick, jerky motions. "Thank God you're here, Sheriff." Her stress level registered in the high pitch of her voice. "They planned it, those girls planned these fires, and God knows what else. I think they would have loved to burn all of Samarcand to the ground."

"Calm down a bit, Miz Mac." the sheriff responded, "we're here now and we'll sort this out. I don't think you have to worry about any more fires. You say the girls started the fires? You have any idea how many and who was involved, especially the leaders?"

"We most certainly do," Agnes said emphatically, reasserting her authority. "We've got a group of them, about twenty, in the conference room down the hall. Miss Stott, Miss Crenshaw and I have been questioning them since right after I called you."

31

"Excuse me, Miss MacNaughton, but how did you pick them out?" Deputy Mudd asked.

"First we brought all the girls from Chamberlain here, then asked any of them that had anything to do with the fires, or knew anything about them, to step into the conference room. Eighteen did. We heard from some of the girls outside that three girls from Bickett had started that fire, and we got those girls as well. I'm pretty sure we have them all, certainly all the ring leaders. We felt we had to isolate those involved from the rest of the residents, that was our chief concern. Otherwise, they could have set even more fires.

"We told them that since a fire, the first fire, began in Chamberlain minutes after the Bickett fire we knew somebody had started it. We told them we had information from some of the girls about who had done it, and they might as well confess. Then Rosa Mull, she's the youngest, spoke up and said she got matches that afternoon from the teacher's room and hid them. Then some of the others spoke up. Margaret Pridgen said she helped set the fires. Later she tried to take the whole blame, said she set a paper dress pattern on fire in her closet. Margaret is a bad apple, Sheriff. She's uppity. "

"You find any evidence the fire at Bickett was set?" asked Deputy Mudd, "Anything soaked in turpentine or kerosene? "

"It was a hot fire, Larry," Agnes snapped, angered by what she took as criticism of her judgment. "Burned so fast nobody could get near the building. Set trees on fire, burned the pine needles. You know how these pine-framed buildings burn. Two girls said Pearl Stiles set it, but she won't admit to it. The Chamberlain fire is different; the girls there are our

32

troublemakers. When something happens at Chamberlain, we know who did it."

"You get any of the girls to write out or sign statements or confessions?" CJ asked.

"I took some notes, as did Miss Stott, but I'm afraid we failed to get the girls to sign anything, didn't think about it, really. Some of them were crying, all excited and scared. Some denied knowing anything. We're pretty sure Margaret Pridgen, Rosa Mull, Marian Mercer, and Ollie Harding set the fires at Chamberlain. They're habitual troublemakers. But we think the twelve other girls also were involved one way or the other. They each indicated they helped obtain matches, or knew about the plan. And we have good reason to think Pearl Stiles set the fire in Bickett. These are the ones we sent to the administration building."

"You tell them what a serious crime they were being accused of, Miz Mac?" asked CJ. "That it's a capital offense?"

"Yes," Agnes replied curtly. "Miss Stott told the girls arson is a capital crime. You can talk with them yourself. They are still there with Miss Stott and Miss Crenshaw." CJ started to ask if she told the girls what a capital crime was, but thought better of it. Instead he and Deputy Mudd followed Agnes into a room filled with girls, silent and sullen, most seated, a few standing nervously close to their accused fellow arsonists. CJ greeted Miss Stott and Miss Crenshaw, but otherwise remained silent, deferring to the superintendent.

"Girls," Agnes addressed the group, "this is Sheriff CJ McDonald, sheriff of Moore County, and his chief deputy, Deputy Mudd." At the mention of his deputy's name, CJ.noticed a smile flicker across the face of one girl, then quickly disappear. "Girls,

they are going to ask you some questions about the fires,"
continued Agnes. "This is serious business, and you are to tell
the whole truth. Lying will only get you in more trouble. Sheriff
McDonald, please proceed."

"If it's all right with you, Miz Mac, Deputy Mudd and I will
move to the back of the room. Please send the girls to us one at a
time. I think we'll start with you, young lady," he said to the girl
who had smirked when she heard Deputy Mudd's name. "Please
follow us."

Surprised to be chosen first, Margaret Pridgen followed the
sheriff and the deputy and sat in a large chair in front of them.
She wasn't afraid and had no intention of lying. This was her
chance to get out of Samarcand and she was determined to take
it. She calmly told how she had set the first fire in Chamberlain
and been disappointed when the staff found and extinguished it.
Then she related how she had set the second, using dress
patterns, watching carefully to make sure the fire caught. The
deputy wrote on a yellow pad while she talked. Margaret
thought he was nice. When he asked her why she did it, she said
because she just felt mean and wanted to get out of Samarcand
and go home. He smiled at that, but it seemed a sad smile. He
told her she could go and thanked her.

Margaret walked to join the other girls, who stood and
watched as Miss MacNaughton sent them one by one to talk with
the sheriff. Marian Mercer went next, then Mary Bronson. As
the girls returned to the group, each whispered answers to the
other girls' whispered questions. Marian said she told the
officers what happened, that she had helped light the first fire,
but knew nothing of the second. Peg seemed completely
bewildered when she returned. When Margaret asked what she
said, she answered simply, "I told them what I did." Ollie

34

Harding, Virginia Hayes, Edna Clark, Mary Bronson, Bertha Hall, Rosa Mull and Estelle Wilson said they admitted to helping find matches or knowing about the fires, but told Sheriff McDonald they did not set any fires, and had only told Miss MacNaughton they knew about the fires in the hope such an admission would get them out of Samarcand.

Pearl Stiles returned to the group indignant. "I told them I didn't do nothing, and I told Miz MacNaughton and Miz Stott I didn't do nothing." Virginia French, Wilma Owens, Chloe Stillwell, and Dolores Seawell all insisted they told the Sheriff they knew nothing about the fires, and had said so to Miss MacNaughton.

After questioning the girls, McDonald and Mudd sat talking for several minutes before walking over to Agnes MacNaughton. "Miz Mac, may we step into your office for a minute?" the sheriff asked. Agnes agreed and led the two men into her office, while the girls remained clustered in the conference room under the watchful eyes of Estelle Stott and Claire Crenshaw. In the office, CJ said, "We have a problem. We can't just take someone into custody without an arrest warrant. None of your staff saw anybody actually set a fire, nor did we. Only four admit to starting the fire in Chamberlain, and the only girl accused of starting the fire in Bickett flatly denies it. In addition to these legal issues, no justice of the peace is available to issue an arrest warrant now. To get an arrest warrant, either you or somebody on your staff is gonna have to go before a judge and take an oath to get cause for an arrest."

"CJ," Agnes interrupted the sheriff, her face flushed and eyes flashing, "I don't care about the niceties of the law. These girls are dangerous. They have burned down two buildings tonight, and you know it. I want them out of here, and I want

35

them out of here tonight. I can't risk the safety of 240 girls. These residences are tinder boxes, and we have every reason to expect some of these girls will make another attempt to burn them. You have to get them out. Now."

"Couldn't we put them in protective custody?" asked the deputy. "That would ease Miz Mac's mind and give us time to sort out the rest later."

What the hell am I going to do with sixteen girls, half of them wearing practically nothing, McDonald thought, but he realized the superintendent faced a dilemma she expected him to solve. "All right, Miz Mac, we can transport them to the jail at Carthage tonight. But there has to be a hearing before a magistrate within the next few days."

"Thank you, Sheriff." Agnes said, her voice thick with relief. "Please make every effort to take them quietly, without disturbing the other girls."

"I understand, We'll do our best."

"Girls," the Sheriff began when he returned to the conference room, "we need to ask you some more questions. It's getting late, and there has been enough excitement here tonight, so we are going to ride you into Carthage. I'd like you girls to step to the front of the room, here next to Deputy Mudd. Just follow the deputy, please. He's going to take you to a bus outside."

Without protest, all sixteen girls fell in line behind the deputy, the sheriff bringing up the rear. "You see," Margaret whispered to Peg in front of her as they marched toward the bus that would deliver them to jail cells, "I told you this would get us out of Samarcand."

36

Agnes MacNaughton watched the girls march quietly out of the conference room into the night to the bus that awaited them. At the sight of CJ McDonald's back disappearing through the doorway, she felt the tension in her body subside. It was over for now, this long night of worry and fear and dread. She felt as if her legs would buckle beneath her. What a welcome back she had received! Better she had stayed away longer. She took a moment to clear her mind and straighten her back, trying not to reveal her momentary loss of composure.

"Estelle, Claire," she heard herself say, "it has been a long evening. Let's get some sleep. The danger appears to be over, though tomorrow will confront us with problems aplenty. Now if you don't mind, I'll say good night." She walked down the corridor to her bedroom and lay upon her bed, shivering in the chill of the room, wondering why she felt so cold when fires still smoldered outside. If only the Samarcand board had approved the request she had made for a better heating system for the buildings, for better fire equipment. Didn't they understand she couldn't perform miracles? Didn't they care how much responsibility she had with limited resources? She took a deep breath, reached for her purse, opened it, and fished out the silver flask.

Ten miles away, Sheriff McDonald and Deputy Mudd marched the girls into the Carthage jail where they were met by jailor Austin Smith, whose family resided on the first floor. Once inside the building, the girls shifted from sullen passivity to vocal resistence. Led by an angelic-faced blonde the sheriff would later learn was Mary Bronson, the girls directed a stream of profanity at the officers which would have done a drunken sailor proud. Damn, thought McDonald, a tough bunch, they did torch the place. He now took MacNaughton's warnings about them seriously and moved to squelch any physical resistance.

37

"That's enough of that," he said, his voice raised but controlled. "You girls have to stay here until we get things sorted out, and if you give us any trouble, I swear I'll put the lot of you in a sweat box. So I want you to follow Mr. Smith here to a cell and go to bed."

His threat reduced the profanity to a few indiscernible mutterings beneath the breath, and the girls fell in line behind the jailor, who led them off. Margaret followed the other girls down a hallway to four cells, and at jailor Smith's bidding entered a cell with Peg, Marian Mercer, and Virginia Hayes. Except for bunk beds anchored to brick walls to the left and right of the door, a sink and a toilet, the cell was empty of furnishings. Virginia and Marian claimed the bottom bunks, as she and Peg clambered up to the top. This was not at all what Margaret had expected, but she and the other girls were exhausted, and she already felt closer to home. The mattresses were somewhat thicker than the ones at Samarcand, and she hoped were without bed bugs. Each mattress was covered with a gray wool blanket, but the cell was so warm she hardly needed it. She crawled under the blanket, slightly alarmed by a strange clinking and clanking which Virginia explained came from pipes carrying steam heat. From somewhere deep inside the building, she could hear noises made by men she could not see. "Good night, Peg," she called, pulled the blanket up to her chin, pushed the voices of the male prisoners from her mind, pretended the noise of the steam pipes was the sound of a Coast Line train taking her back home, and slept.

The next morning the jailer brought a breakfast of warm oatmeal and milk, but no news as to when Margaret and the others might be going home or anywhere else. She could hear the twelve girls in the three other cells talking about what might

38

happen next, and none had the faintest idea. Virginia said it might take awhile before the sheriff could figure out what to do with them, to which Margaret replied she was certain her family would come as soon as they learned of her predicament, and they must regret sending her away. This upset Peg, who began to cry because she had no family to claim her. Margaret calmed her down, saying the sheriff would know what to do, and switched the subject to last night's fires. The girls rehashed the events. Lunch was a peanut butter and jelly sandwich and more milk, but they received no further information. As the afternoon dragged by, the girls entertained each other with counting games and fantastic tales of what they planned to do once they were free. Supper was a meal of beans and rice and a biscuit, but no meat, and still no information. The girls ate in silence, Peg breaking into tears occasionally, and went to bed as soon as it was dark. There were no bedbugs.

Soon after the jailer delivered their oatmeal and milk the following morning, Sheriff McDonald appeared. "Girls," he said, "as soon as you finish eating, I want you to wash up a bit. We're going to take you to Magistrate Humber. He'll ask you some questions before we can decide what to do with you, and I want you to be truthful with him. This is important. Now get ready, and I'll be back in a few minutes."

The girls washed their faces, pressed down their hair, and straightened their clothes as best they could in preparation for the next step in the journey which none of them understood. Margaret used a comb she found in her dress pocket, then ran the comb through Peg's thoroughly tangled thin blonde strands, finishing just as the jailer opened the cell doors. Once again the girls followed Deputy Mudd and the sheriff, who were now joined by a matron, into the bus for the short ride to the court house.

The matron and Deputy Mudd ushered them into the chambers of Magistrate George W. Humber and seated them before a rather young but balding man dressed in a dark suit and tie. Margaret was surprised to see that Agnes MacNaughton, Estelle Stott, Claire Crenshaw, and Judy Ross were also in the room.

George McNeil watched the girls file into the magistrate's courtroom, a forlorn group, silent, unsmiling, looking even younger than when he had first seen them twenty-four hours earlier in the Moore County jail. The half-hour visit had yielded little useful information, except for the fact that all the girls except Margaret Pridgen and Thelma Edna Clark adamantly denied any involvement with the Samarcand fires. George had been appointed by the district court to represent them, for reasons not explained and he could not fathom, and he had agreed to take them on. As the girls were seated behind him on courtroom benches, he prepared to muster routine objections to their arrest and appearance before George Humber, objections which he had realized from the time of his appointment would prove futile.

The District Court had appointed him, George suspected, because it wanted a local attorney to defend the girls, and his suspicions proved partially correct. The State had wanted a local attorney, someone well regarded but an average man, without a high profile. He was perfect for the role, all-around average, average height and weight, average appearance, average brown hair and brown eyes, nothing to distinguish him from any of the suited men who plied their trade in the courtrooms of Moore and surrounding counties and lived in neat bungalows just off the main streets of Carthage or Troy. He was an average attorney, competent but not brilliant before the bench and juries.

The appearance of the prosecutor, who was not from a local or district court, reaffirmed George's sense that the hearing's outcome was a foregone conclusion. The State Attorney General's office had dispatched a prosecutor down from Raleigh to handle the case. Not just any staffer, but Walter Siler, one of North Carolina's most noted legal minds and mentor to many aspiring bright young Raleigh attorneys. A handsome man, wearing a flawlessly tailored navy pinstripe suit, Siler looked the part of a high-powered state attorney. This case, George thought, is going to generate some publicity, and Raleigh wants to make sure the publicity does the state no harm. He complimented himself on accepting the case, realizing this publicity would reflect on him. In these tough economic times, any attention was welcome.

George walked over to Siler, whom he had met twice before. "Hello, Walter," he said, "I'm George McNeil, appointed for the defense. We've met before, both times in Raleigh. Welcome to Moore County." He extended his hand.

"Yes, of course I remember." Siler grasped George's hand, and official smile flickering across his face but his eyes were not smiling. "Can't say I'm happy to be here, under the circumstances."

"And I can't say I blame you for feeling that way," George replied. "Not much good likely to come out of this." He wondered whether Siler really remembered him, as he took his seat and watched Siler call his witnesses. The hearing, as he had anticipated, went quickly. Agnes MacNaughton, Estelle Stott, and Sheriff McDonald recounted their roles in questioning the girls. Both MacDonald and Stott insisted that almost all the girls had indicated their participation in the arson, and that existed corroborating testimony from other residents that those

41

who denied involvement were lying. McDonald had little to add, and only confirmed the statements of MacNaughton and Stott.

The rules of a probable cause hearing precluded George from calling witnesses and presenting evidence, although he was allowed to cross-examine the State's witnesses. He quickly determined that an aggressive challenge to their testimony would be ineffective and very likely to irritate the magistrate. He briefly questioned MacNaughton and Stott, asking whether either had actually seen any of the girls set fires, to which he received a negative response. Within less than an hour the hearing was over. Humber ruled the State had amply proved probably cause, and he bound the girls over for trial in the May term of the Moore County Superior Court, on the charge of first degree arson.

The hearing over, Sheriff McDonald approached Agnes MacNaughton and Estelle Stott. "Well, Miz Mac, you've got your wish," he said, an indictment for first degree arson for all sixteen girls. No need to worry what else they might do, they won't be going back to Samarcand. The Attorney General's Office has arranged for them to be taken to the Robeson County jail in Lumberton . Sheriff Kornegay has agreed to house them until they can be tried. My jail is too small and not equipped to handle many female prisoners. The Lumberton jail has a female wing, and he'll put them there. Of course, the trial, whenever it is held, will be in Moore County Courthouse in Carthage. I expect I'll see you several times before the trial date."

"Thank you, CJ," a relieved Agnes MacNaughton replied. "I hope I didn't seem too demanding last night, but I was truly concerned for the rest of the residents. These girls are dangerous. You best keep a close watch on them. There's no telling what they're capable of. I am, I must admit, delighted they will be gone from Samarcand, although I am not looking forward to a trial."

"I understand completely, Miz Mac," the sheriff assured her. "This has been a bizarre episode, especially troubling for you, I'm sure. I for one hope the trial is held soon and over quickly. Meanwhile, I have to transport these girls to Lumberton and Sheriff Kornegay. I'll be happy to turn them over to him."

Back on the bus, the girls remained silent under the watchful eyes of the matron and Sheriff McDonald, while Deputy Mudd drove. Within moments Margaret realized they were not returning to the Carthage jail, but instead were headed east. Perhaps, she hoped, they were headed to Wilmington, reversing the route which had brought her to Samarcand. As the drive began, only a few whimpers broke the silence. But the mood soon lightened and an excited buzz filled the bus as the girls speculated about their destination. Within an hour, the bus was making its way through the streets of Lumberton, a larger and busier community than Carthage, and the girls again fell silent as they watched the townscape drift by. The bus pulled to a stop before a large building with a big white sign announcing it was the Robeson County Jail. Margaret read the sign and forgot about Wilmington.

The Riot

At least, Margaret thought, this new jail was much better than the one in Carthage. The bunks were the same, but the cells were larger, with two chairs and a small table. Since they occupied five of the seven cells on the women's wing, the girls enjoyed considerably more space, and the women's wing gave them additional privacy. The food was better, too, eggs and bacon for breakfast, and meat with supper. Margaret wound up in a cell with Marian Mercer and Virginia Hayes, both of whom she liked. She missed rooming with Peg, but could still talk with her easily since she was placed in a cell next door. For the first few days, the girls were glad to be away from Samarcand. A group of ladies from the Lumberton Woman's Club visited, bringing clothes and personal items—combs, soap, toothbrushes, and toothpaste. The women continued to visit once or twice a week, helping the girls try on new outfits and new hair styles. Margaret participated in these jail cell fashion shows, but without much enthusiasm. Most of the other girls looked forward to the women's visits. Others preferred to write letters home since someone anonymously had established a stamp and stationery fund. Margaret wrote occasionally, receiving replies from her grandmother or father, and she felt sorry for Peg and some of the others who had no family. Visits from newspaper reporters, some from as far away as Raleigh, occasionally broke their routine. Margaret talked with several of them, always telling exactly how she had set the fires in Chamberlain, which seemed to amaze them. Margaret enjoyed the attention.

When time seemed to drag, several of the girls would suggest some activity to keep up their spirits. Always the most imaginative, Mary Lee Bronson staged a talent show, featuring herself. Dressed in her best outfit, she presented herself as a young Jean Harlow. Not to be outdone, Marian Mercer picked out a more revealing dress and pretended she was Clara Bow. When the fashion game grew boring, the girls found other means of entertaining themselves. Dolores Stillwell and Estelle Wilson liked to dance with Mary Lee singing the tunes, while the other girls paired up and giggled through the Charleston or the fox trot. Edna Clark and Virginia Hayes led in singing rounds, which Margaret enjoyed, especially the dirty verses Peg and Wilma Owens had a knack for creating, and they all soon learned by heart. Unless they became overly boisterous, the jail's matron never interfered, no matter how raucous or bawdy the songs. In fact, Margaret saw the matron tapping her feet to the music.

But as the days passed into weeks, time began to drag. Some club women continued to visit, bringing new clothes and toiletries, but even those occasions lost appeal. The occasional reporter dropped in, breaking the monotony, but these visits were few and far between. Despite the best efforts of her cell mates to rally the group's spirits, Margaret felt her hopes declining. According to Mary Lee and some of the older girls, they were going to have to go to court and be tried for arson sometime, but they didn't know when. One thing for sure, she wasn't going home until after the trial, and depending on what happened, perhaps not at all. After almost a month in jail, Margaret was desperate to get out and prepared to take any action that might get her sent home.

"Marian," she said one morning, "let's start another fire. That way they'll have to let us go."

"Are you sure?" Marian asked. "It didn't work out so well the last time."

"I'm sure I don't want to stay here, in this jail day after day, no telling when we'll get out. I can't see how anything could be much worse than this. I want some fresh air. At least we can create some excitement. You'd like a little excitement, wouldn't you? You willing to help or not?"

"I will if Virginia will."

"Why the hell not?" said Virginia. "Who's got some matches?"

"Wilma Owens, she's a smoker, always got matches," Margaret said. "She's next door with Josephine, Dolores, and Rosa. Let's ask her." "Yeah, go ahead and ask her," Marian agreed.

Margaret called out, "Wilma, you got any matches?"

"Yeah, why?"

"We need some excitement," laughed Margaret.

"Sounds good to me," Wilma said, "here they come." A box of matches came sliding down the floor, and Margaret reached between the bars to drag them inside her cell.

"I've got another box. Let's see what you can do, and we'll MATCH you," Wilma laughed.

"Pull off your blankets and set them on top of the mattresses. That ought to make a quick fire," Margaret advised Marian and Virginia, who obeyed. Within seconds the girls had all four bunks ablaze.

"Fire! Fire!" they yelled and pounded on the cell door, making as much of a racket as possible. Margaret looked down the hall and saw smoke coming from Wilma's cell, and heard the

46

other girls screaming, "Fire! " and beating on their cell doors, until the noise reverberated throughout the cell block.

"Let's give them a real show, tear this damn place apart." She grabbed a chair, and shrieking at the top of her lungs, she smashed it into a bunk bed. Marian and Virginia quickly joined in, dancing and howling as they hurled piece after piece of furniture, splintering them to bits.

"Let's break some glass," Virginia yelled. She picked up pieces of shattered furniture and threw them into the windows and light fixtures, thrilling to the sound of breaking glass. She heard the crash of more broken furniture and glass next door as Wilma and the others joined in the rampage.

Caught up in the frenzy, Margaret failed to hear jailor Austin Smith and the matron running down the corridor. "You girls stop this, stop it right now," she heard Smith yell. Smith unlocked the cell and moved toward the girls, the matron right behind him. Marion picked up a chair rung and flung it at the officers.

"Get the hell out of here!" Marion yelled.

Margaret glimpsed Smith grab Marion as she reached for another chair rung. "Leave her alone," Margaret screamed at Smith just as the matron tackled Margaret about the waist, driving her to the floor. Sheriff Kornegay and four other deputies arrived, entering the cell next door where Wilma greeted one of the deputies with a plate full of food in his face.

The girls continued to kick, bite, and scratch, but were no match for the stronger men. Subdued by force, they were escorted to the runaround, the exercise area for longterm prisoners, to remove the girls from the smoke in the cells. By now the Lumberton fire department had arrived, pulled their hoses into the cells, and begun to extinguish the still-smouldering bedding and mattresses. With the girls and fires under control, Sheriff Kornegay ordered a large fireproof cell at the center of the jail prepared for the seven rebellious girls, all furniture removed and the iron bunks stripped of mattresses and bedding.

Overpowered but unyielding, the girls found a way to strike back. They managed to do what the usual drunken occupants of their cells had never done—removed strips of iron from their bunks, which for three nights and days they used to beat against the cell walls and bunk frames to torment their captors and deny them rest. Sheriff Kornegay finally had enough, and appealed to the Attorney General's Office to have the girls shipped to Central Prison in Raleigh. His request refused, he placed a call to Sheriff McDonald.

"CJ, I know I said I'd hold the Samarcand girls for you until the trial, but as you know, some of them tried to burn down my jail, fought with my deputies when we tried to stop them. In the three nights since, they've continued to make such a racket my jailor and his family can't sleep. That Margaret Pridgen, she seems to be the leader in this, is a little hellion, and so are some of the others. Sorry, CJ, but I want them out of my jail, and the State won't take them. I've got seven of them locked up in a cell, no bedding, no furniture, nothing they can possibly set on fire. I'd appreciate it if you could get them out of here today."

Two hours later, the Moore County bus with Sheriff McDonald, Deputy Mudd and two additional deputies, arrived at the Robeson County jail. Margaret, Marian, Wilma, Virginia, Rosa, Dolores, and Josephine were immediately loaded onto the bus for the return trip to the Moore County jail. Quiet

48

desperation settled upon the girls left in Lumberton. A few weeks later, a despondent Pearl Stiles wrote to plead with the governor of North Carolina, himself the owner of a textile mill, to intervene on her own behalf and that of the other eight girls still incarcerated in the Lumberton jail:

> Dear Governor Gardner,
>
> The way we were treated was terrible. We were locked, beat, and fed on bread and water most of the time. We girls in Roberson County Jail is just as innocent of this crime they hold against us as a little child. Please give me liberty or death. Mr. Gardner, this is Pearl Stiles writing and I am always trying to be good. Please pardon us 8 Girls in Roberson County Jail and help us to get out of this trouble if you wish to. So we can go back home to our Parents those who have them. And the ones who hasn't any parents can be adopted out to people.
>
> I didn't have one thing to do with that old fire. Well all the girls said to give you their love for them. Will close with good heart.
>
> From Miss Pearl Stiles to Mr. Gardner.
>
> Lumberton, North Carolina. Answer at once."

Pearl never received an answer.

2

The Decision

Carrying a sack of file folders, Cornelia Battle Lewis emerged from the red brick Briggs Hardware store on Fayetteville Street across from her law office, on the sixth floor of the National Banking and Trust building at the corner of Martin Street in downtown Raleigh, North Carolina. As she entered the post office in the next block, a gust of wind blew her short brown hair into her eyes. The weather had been fair and mild in the morning when she left the home she built near St. Mary's College with money from her father's estate. Now the temperature was dropping. She considered stopping by Moore Square to purchase a small chicken and collards for supper, perhaps to serve with boiled potatoes. Then she remembered it was a Wednesday and the city market was only open a half day. Never mind. After long hours organizing her new law office, preparing a meal for just one person was a chore she could do without. Perhaps she would stop by the Mecca restaurant around the corner, opened by a friendly Greek immigrant named Nick, and order a meat and macaroni pie. She liked the place, with its diamond-pattern tile floor and cozy wooden booths. Already the Mecca was a magnet for the wheeling and dealing and gossip of the capital city's lawyers and politicians. Sometimes she took breakfast there.

But she didn't feel up to socializing; she would be better off lighting a fire and sipping sherry while she ruminated on her March 15, 1931, "Incidentally" column published a week earlier in the Raleigh *News and Observer*. This column on the deaths of black prisoners because of dangerous jail conditions had immediately provoked criticism. She would measure the worth of her words by the number of irate letters she received from readers who supported the status quo. She found writing her Sunday column in the state's premier newspaper to be the most satisfying work she had ever undertaken. She was grateful to publisher Josephus Daniels and his son, editor Jonathan Daniels, for providing her the opportunity to air her views and stir up the readership.

"Afternoon, Nell," said the postmaster, holding out a thick packet of mail wrapped in a paper band marked NBL. "I see you've gored a few more oxen." Nell smiled. Her column was hitting its mark. "Want to fill out a change of address for your office? 'Bout time. Been there most a month."

"Tomorrow," Nell said. "Right now I've one more letter to write." Recrossing Fayetteville Street against the light, she dodged a WPTF radio truck headed north to Capitol Square. Lucky it didn't hit me, she thought, remembering that the station's call letters stood for We Protect The Family. Two years earlier, in the Ruffin Building which faced the capitol, she had taken her oral exams before the justices of the State Supreme Court and had been admitted to the Bar. Now, entering the bank building, she sneezed as she thumbed through her packet of mail. Her brief foray out of doors, the wind blowing pollen from the canopy of Capitol Square oaks, must have activated the sinus condition which flared from time to time to create an annoying sweet taste which no amount of oral hygiene could overcome. As she made her way to her office, she stopped by the restroom to rinse out her mouth. Two secretaries were talking in loud whispers in the hall, blocking the restroom door. "Nine of them," one was saying. " Heard it on the radio. Nine Nigras over in Alabama, raped two white girls today in a freight car."

The other secretary's eyes were wide. "Catch 'em yet?"

"Got 'em up at Scottsboro."

"Probably lynch 'em."

The secretaries moved aside to allow Nell to enter the restroom. "Sorry, Miss Lewis," they said in unison.

Nell's lips tightened. "I would wait to make a judgment in this matter until you have heard the facts. A news bulletin sensationalizes such events." She hid the curiosity instigated by their conversation and decided to go directly to her office, write her last letter of the day, then head home quickly to listen to the evening news. Nine Negroes. Two white women. In the Deep South. Alabama. If true, this would be a sensational case indeed. A prosecuting attorney and a defense attorney could build a lifelong reputation out of such an event. "Bear in mind," she said to the secretaries, "these men are presumed innocent until proved guilty."

The secretaries rolled their eyes. "Yes, ma'am." Nell walked briskly down the hall, heard them giggle, and glanced back over her shoulder to see them twirl their index fingers at their temples.

Shutting her office door with a firm snap which echoed down the hall, Nell set the packet of mail on a corner of the desk which had been her late father's, and arranged the folders from Briggs Hardware in her file cabinet for alphabetizing when she organized the papers and documents stacked on the long mahogany table she had liberated from her parental home at Cloverdale. She wished she could afford a secretary to handle the multitude of tedious clerical tasks which diluted the exhilaration of practicing law, but the stock market crash had diminished her financial resources, and until she derived income from her new profession she must limit monthly expenditures. Besides, dealing with secretaries such as those she had just encountered would have tried her patience beyond endurance. She realized these young women likely occupied a social stratum which limited their cultural awareness. Drawn to the capital city from nearby small towns like Zebulon and Wendell, they took classes in stenography and typing at the business school and sought broader horizons through employment with banks and local attorneys, or perhaps snared a plum intermittent job serving in the secretarial pool at the biennial General Assembly. The prettier ones would catch a husband and settle into domesticity, while the less appealing would never marry and spend their lives as some married boss's office-wife.

Other than lower social pedigree by virtue of birth into the Southern caste system, were these women so different from Nell herself? She regretted being short with them. She had been on her own life odyssey, escaping the provincialism of her hometown for greener pastures at Smith College, adventuring into YMCA canteen service in France in World War One, studying law briefly at Columbia in New York City, campaigning for a seat in the state legislature. Not to mention her youthful anticipation of marriage to Lenoir Chambers, whom she had loved passionately and for whom she still secretly carried the torch. She sublimated her unfulfilled libido in devotion to volunteerism and social causes, sought to alleviate her underlying depression through religious study, allowed herself to be medicated and psychoanalyzed by physicians at institutions recommended by her family patriarchy, and threw herself into new pursuits such as organizing this very law office.

What a hypocrite she was! She dreaded the end of day, fast approaching, when she would return to the solitude of her home, no one there to welcome her, no husband for whom to prepare chicken and collards while they engaged in serious or trivial conversation. This was her truth. Since her highest value was avoiding self-deception, she forced herself to honestly face her own demons. How else could she maintain integrity as she went about critiquing others in her column?

Restless, she walked over to the window and looked down upon the deepening shadows of Fayetteville Street. Picking up three books from the mahogany table, she placed them, one by one, on the empty bookshelf behind her desk. She arranged Pearl Buck's latest novel *The Good Earth* next to Buck's novel *East Wind, West Wind*, and remembered the author's admonition that the person who tries to live alone will not succeed as a human being, for the heart withers if it does not answer another heart. She sighed, wondering whether Lenoir Chambers had found true happiness with the widowed Greensboro society editor he had married two years earlier.

She put on the bookshelf her prized autographed copy of her Carolina Playmakers friend Paul Green's celebrated drama *In Absalom's Bosom*. She missed performing in theatre, as she had done as a student at St. Mary's School and Smith College. But delivering a jury speech as a trial attorney would utilize her dramatic talents. She had bought the newly-published Buck novel as a present to herself on Valentine's Day, from the Intimate Bookshop in Chapel Hill. The bookshop was little more than a dorm room inhabited by two students who were disciples of Green, but she anticipated that in time the venture would flourish and she wished to lend her support as a charter customer.

Chapel Hill afforded relief from the social customs of Old Raleigh into which she had been born, and the state politics which permeated the capital city. Chapel Hill also had its politics, to be sure, and they often overlapped, but there was less horse trading and more clash of stimulating ideas. A pleasurable aspect of her Hill visits was walking beneath the trees in Battle Park, sensing the spiritual presence of her half-brothers' grandfather Kemp Plummer Battle, who served admirably as UNC president for fifteen years and nurtured this woodsy mid-campus area. She also could not deny that here she felt in communion with Lenoir Chambers, who graduated from the university in 1914, the year World War One began. In a private place in her home she had tucked away the poem she penned for Lenoir in Nice, France, in another March a dozen years earlier: "I wonder what they hold for us, those years ahead we talk about; and if a length of common days shall see fires, leaping now, die out; and shall I ever find you old, and will Time put our dreams to rout?"

How happy she had been with Lenoir, filled with the passion of youth, before Time doused their romantic dreams. How angry she had felt with her father and brothers when she suspected that behind her back they had warned Lenoir she might have inherited her mother's tendency to melancholy, which she could pass on to her children. If they had, as she had good reason to believe, it amounted to a conspiracy to violate her right of self-determination and demonstrated the sense of male entitlement to control the lives of females, as if she were the property of her father and brothers. As an unmarried woman she was in large measure financially dependent upon the male members of her family, and must hold in check her instinct to rail at them for interfering in her personal affairs. She also believed they had her best interests at heart.

To further complicate matters, she felt conflicted about Lenoir Chambers. Their passion for each other had been apparent, their mutual interests compatible, and their future together a foregone conclusion when he abruptly withdrew. If he had truly loved her as she did him, he would have stood his ground and refused to be dissuaded. He would have forthrightly discussed the situation with her and made a mutual decision to proceed or end their engagement. She wished she could entirely put him out of her mind and heart, but some part of her hoped he would admire her achievements and her courage in challenging the status quo, and he would feel a tinge of regret in having abandoned her. Oh my! That word abandonment had crept into her psychoanalytical sessions when she discussed the loss of her mother. Nell had protested that it was not her mother's intention to die, but her psychiatrist had pointed out that as a child Nell might have blamed herself for her mother's going away, and when her fiancé Lenoir also took his leave, this might have reawakened her childhood sorrow.

But her experience with Gastonia's Loray Mill strikers caused her to realize she was among the blessed, with an excellent education and family connections providing access to the movers and shakers in North Carolina. She took Christ's message to heart, believing she had a duty to the less fortunate. Today, rather than indulge in self-pity she would make the most of her freedom to follow her own instincts. She would put her office in order and write her letter regarding the unusual case which promised to be significant in the annals of North Carolina jurisprudence. Sixteen adolescent girls had been incarcerated in Moore County jail on March 12, charged with the death penalty for collectively committing arson at the state reform school for wayward white girls, a place identified by the exotic name Samarcand Manor. News stories described the perpetrators as girls of a lower social caste than the secretaries in the hall of Nell's office building, and certainly far beneath her own privileged status as a daughter of Southern aristocracy.

Nell realized that if she accepted this case, it would be fraught with complications and provide little or no financial compensation to offset her expenses. Bleeding heart Nell, she thought ruefully. Perhaps she did indeed have a Jesus martyr complex, as suggested by one psychiatrist. But never mind. She was tempted by the opportunity to defend these underprivileged girls against the excesses of a system biased against them. After all, she herself had recommended creation of just such a place for troubled youth. In 1917 the state legislature established the State Home and Industrial School for Girls, an institution for "wayward girls and fallen women." A. A. McGeachy, a member of the State House from Charlotte and a Presbyterian minister, had introduced the legislation, and, along with other reform-minded legislators and the considerable lobbying power of the North Carolina Federation of Women's Clubs, seen to its passage. The newly-formed school on 300 acres was named after Samarkand Farms, the residence of Moore County's wealthy Raphael W. Pumpelly Jr., who had traveled with his father to the ancient city Samarkand on Asia's historic Silk Road. The site had previously been the private Marienfeld Outdoor-Air School for Boys. In 1931, Samarcand housed 275 inmates as wards of the state, where they might receive vocational training and practical experience in healthy surroundings. Years before, using her newspaper column to journalistically light fires in the arid North Carolina intellectual landscape, she herself had proclaimed that the solution to the forward movement of women would be a smashed window or two, along with a little arson.

Lacking her literacy and the capital city newspaper as a forum, these girls had made use of the only weapon at their disposal, striking a match to make their disgruntlements manifest, in the institution under the auspices of the State Board of Charities and Welfare for which Nell had served as publicity chairman. Five years earlier, she had praised Samarcand's superintendent Agnes MacNaughton for fostering good spirit among the residents of the institution. Beyond this, in a fanciful frame of mind, she had composed a poem describing how "the dancing girls of Samarcand float in the mists of fairyland." What could have prompted such a large group of them to rebel in such a dramatic and destructive way? The school's avowed purpose was to improve the lives of girls and young women, but in the bucolic sandhills only two hour's drive from Raleigh, as the peach trees were budding, something had gone terribly awry.

Nell spied a patch of broken plaster above her file cabinets. Before she wrote her letter, she would cover this blemish. With a small hammer and a nail from Briggs Hardware she affixed to the wall her framed cartoon published in the *News and Observer*, mocking an executive of the Loray Mill in Gastonia. The executive wore a top-hat and was smoking a cigar as he held up a Confederate battle flag labelled "states' rights," played off against a woman mill worker holding an infant and a child mill worker. The cartoon embodied the issues in the Loray Mill Strike which began April 1, 1929, during which the National Textile Workers Union was at loggerheads with anti-union

59

forces. Covering the story as a journalist, Nell has learned firsthand the extremes to which the machinery of the state would go to protect the privilege of those its economic and political leaders deemed the natural leadership class.

She witnessed militia units ordered to duty by North Carolina Governor O. Max Gardner, ostensibly to protect the mill owners' property from potential violence by strikers, but instead protecting strike-breakers and the gangs of deputized thugs who harassed striking workers. The deputies threw fifty strikers, mostly women and children protesting inhumane conditions, into jail, then moved to evict workers from company-owned housing. In violence instigated by the deputies, Gastonia's police chief Orville Arberholt was killed. In September, union organizer and balladeer Ella Mae Wiggins, mother of nine, was ambushed, shot, and killed. No one was ever charged with her murder or other crimes against the strikers and union organizers. Seven union organizers, identified at their trial as members of the Communist party, were eventually convicted of Arberholt's murder on questionable evidence and sentenced to up to twenty years at hard labor. In vain, Nell used her column to argue for a change of venue for the trial, and to assail the guilty verdict. Nailing up the cartoon, Nell smiled wryly and remembered how Gastonia had pulled in its welcome mat when she went to the jail to interview the women inmates but was turned away.

Next to the cartoon she hung her license to practice law in North Carolina. Yes, she had made the right choice in spending three years reading law, adding this expertise to her journalistic skills as she continued her crusade to better society. It had been a pleasurable experience, reading law under Walter Siler, then in his late forties and still strikingly handsome. Walter had entered politics as the mayor of Siler City, served in several sessions of the state legislature, as a judicial district solicitor, and superior court judge. A reputation as a legal scholar earned him an appointment as Assistant Attorney General in 1927. Well known and well liked by the Raleigh legal and political establishment, he had been the perfect mentor. Nell admired his wit and good looks and only mildly lamented the fact he was married.

She hadn't needed to become a lawyer to advance her journalistic career, but passing the bar examination had given her tremendous satisfaction. Opposed by the North Carolina legislature, the right to vote had only been allowed women since 1920, coming fifteen years after her mother's death in 1895 at age thirty-four. Now age thirty-eight, Nell had already outlived her mother by four years. She felt a moral duty to make the most of the opportunity her mother had been denied, to participate in public life as an enfranchised member of the larger community. How she wished she had known her mother! The conversations they might have had as Nell explored the world! Would her mother have been proud of Nell's graduating Phi Beta Kappa from Smith College? She hoped so. Would her mother have approved of her YMCA canteen work in France during World War One or her work for women's suffrage after the war? She hoped so. Would her mother have been disappointed by Nell's failure to enter domestic life through marriage to Lenoir Chambers, have viewed her daughter as a "fallen woman" because she, an unmarried woman, had engaged in a passionate affair? Nell hoped not.

But her mother had been portrayed with piety akin to sainthood, serving as a Sunday School teacher at Christ Episcopal Church, only a few blocks from Nell's law office. Prior to meeting Nell's widowed father, Dr. Richard Lewis, at the church, Mary Gordon had contemplated entering a convent. Perhaps her mother might have lived much longer as a nun, never experiencing the ill health which followed Nell's birth. In her childhood's darkest moments, Nell indeed had wondered whether she might have been in some way responsible for her mother's death. She sometimes had noticed her father gazing at his only daughter with an expression which implied Nell had an obligation to justify her existence.

A vague image of the woman who had borne her was occasionally dislodged from her memory, accompanied by a faint sweet scent which would linger for a moment and then disappear. With Mary Gordon Lewis' death when Nell was only two, her primary maternal figure became former slave Margaret Selby, whom she called "Mammy," but Mammy, too, had died before Nell reached adolescence. Three half-brothers, Ivey, Kemp, and Richard, were from her father's first marriage to Cornelia Battle, after whom Nell was named. Though the Battle name served well because of its celebrated provenance, and her mother must have approved the name when Nell was baptized at Christ Church, Nell felt the name was disloyal to her mother, who had only one child to carry on her bloodline. Cornelia Lewis had birthed not only Nell's half-brothers, but also a daughter, named Martha but called Pattie. Pattie had died soon after marriage, of illness associated with pregnancy, when Nell was in adolescence. The illness and death of her mother, and of Nell's pregnant half-sister, caused her to pay particular notice to the Episcopal prayer called the Churching of Women, which invokes God's protection during the great pain and peril of childbirth. But her mother's piety had not been her salvation.

Nell disliked her father's third wife, Annie Blackwell, whom she regarded as domineering, narrow-minded, and materialistic, favoring her own son from a prior marriage. Nell could not identify with this woman who took her mother's place when Nell was four years old. Fortuitously, in her sophomore year at St. Mary's School, she found a role model in a new French instructor named Georgina Kellogg. A graduate of Smith College, before coming to St. Mary's the teacher had lived in New York City and spent considerable time in Europe, and was Nell's inspiration to also pursue education at Smith and venture abroad. Nell smiled as she recalled watching Miss Kellogg sew during Sunday services at St. Mary's Chapel, accomplishing something useful while the pontificating droned on around her. Little wonder she lasted only two years at St. Mary's and was gone before Nell's graduation! From a carton of books in a corner of the room, Nell retrieved volumes of St. Mary's yearbook *Muse*, of which she had been editor-in-chief, and placed them on the shelf next to *Absalom's Bosom*.

With each addition to the furnishings of her law office, she felt more confidence in her ability to make her professional mark as a sole practitioner. She was glad she could proceed without being hampered by the needs and wishes of a husband and children. She could arrive early and work late, take her meals at restaurants, travel at will, represent whomever she chose, so long as she managed her office overhead. She was emerging from the malaise which had overcome her after a jury convicted the Loray Mill union organizers of second-degree murder in Chief Arberholt's death, followed by society's failure to prosecute anyone for the ambush and murder of Ella Mae Wiggins. She used her *Incidentally* column of October 27, 1929, to express the bitter lessons learned in Gastonia: "To hell with the orderly processes of civil government which men have set up for their mutual protection! To hell with the ideal of justice....To hell with the theory of democracy in which the rights of the poor and humble are equal to those of the rich and the proud!"

Despite her spirited proclamations in print, the injustice she witnessed in Gastonia, the exploitation of women and children, the triumph of money and power over the rights of the common man, had discouraged her, and the enormous investment of her physical and psychic energy in reporting that prolonged struggle had left her exhausted. She imagined this to be similar to postpartum weakness and depression experienced after pregnancy and childbirth, the anticipation of bringing new life into the world followed by depletion of one's bodily reserves. This sacrifice reminded her of the words of the Episcopal communion ritual: "This is my body which is broken for you." For a few months she had felt broken, in need of respite, perhaps just as her mother had needed respite after Nell's birth, and Nell had sought refuge with her brother Ivey in Charlottesville, Virginia, where she could obtain the recommended abdominal surgery. She was reluctant to become what was medically termed a female castrate through process of ovariectomy, which would necessitate female hormone replacement. But she realized that at her age she was unlikely to ever have children, and marriage was not on her horizon. Back home in Raleigh, recovered from her medical procedures, she could turn her attention with renewed energy to the practice of law.

The end of day was fast approaching, and she had yet to write her letter concerning the arson girls incarcerated in the Moore County jail. Turning on her desk lamp, she took from its envelope a letter addressed to her from former Samarcand registered nurse Viola Sistare, dated four days earlier, March 21, 1931, and postmarked Scranton, Pennsylvania. Miss Sistare explained that she had left employment at Samarcand only ten days before the fires, objecting to the abusive treatment of inmates by administrators. She wrote that she did not blame the girls for rebelling and setting fires in the belief they would be sent home, for she herself had been eager to put the place behind her. Next to Miss Sistare's letter Nell arranged in chronological order news clippings about the arson case, beginning with the Wilmington *Morning Star* dated March 17, which noted that a Wilmington girl, fifteen-year-old Margaret Pridgen, was among the sixteen defendants charged with the capital offense of arson.

The March 17 *News and Observer* revealed that news of the fires was not announced until March 16 when Walter Siler of the state Attorney General's Office arrived in Carthage to help prosecute the cases, and George W. McNeill of Carthage had been appointed defense attorney. The March 18 paper stated that Margaret Pridgen had acknowledged her part in setting fire to the two buildings which housed eighty girls, as had defendants Wilma Owens of Waynesville, Margaret Mercer of Ayden, Mary Lee Bronson of Rocky Mount, Dolores Sewell of Cove City, Thelma Council of Tarboro, Virginia Hayes of Leaksville, Rosa Mull of Rutherford, Edna Clark of Halifax, Pearl Stiles of Canton, Ollie Harding of Washington, Margaret Abernethy of Kinston, Estelle Wilson of Lexington, Chloe Stillwell of Kinston, Josephine French of Haw River, and Bertha Hall of Norfolk, Virginia. A pretty good cross-section of North Carolina, thought Nell. Waywardness seemed not to be confined to only one or two regions of the state, but apparently flourished from the mountains to the sea.

The March 23 Lumberton newspaper *The Robesonian* especially attracted her attention, for it cited the Pridgen girl as taking the entire responsibility for the fires, quoting her that she would "do it again." Though the unrepentant confession would not serve Margaret well as a defendant, Nell felt a kinship with this girl, admiring her rebellious spirit so much like Nell's own.

"She gave as her reason that she was tired of the place and thought she might be moved if the buildings were burned," stated the article. "She says she set fire to Chamberlain Hall after attempts of the other girls to commit the same offense had been halted."

Margaret was described as "scantily clad" as a "cigarette rolled out on the floor under the bed on which she as sitting." The girls "begged matches, cigarettes, magazines, newspapers or stationery." They were characterized as "carefree and happy" and not "realizing the seriousness of the offense with which they were charged." This should be no surprise, thought Nell, because even the best-educated adolescents could not be expected to know the North Carolina penal code, and they were unaware of their own mortality, believing they would live forever despite risky behavior. She found herself looking forward to meeting self-described ringleader Pridgen in person.

With this background, Nell finally could focus on her task at hand, replying to the letter she had just received from her friend, Mrs. Thomas E. Williams of Leaksville. Referring to Margaret Pridgen, Mrs. Williams had written, "I cannot feel that this child and her unfortunate companions are the hardened criminals that this charge would indicate and believe that they should have legal council, who will give their case a more thorough investigation and deeper interest than it could in court." An offer of a small retainer fee accompanied the letter. Nell was glad Mrs. Williams' concern for Margaret was extended to the other defendants, for Virginia Hayes was from Leaksville, and her father W. T. Hayes had made it known Virginia's family did not have the means to employ a private attorney.

The more Nell learned about the Samarcand arson, the more she was inclined to say damn the torpedoes and represent the miscreants. She wished she had someone with whom to explore the ramifications of signing on as co-counsel. If she had a husband at home, she could discuss with him the pros and cons over supper before writing her letter accepting or rejecting the case. Her close friend, Kate Burr Johnson, the first woman appointed director of the North Carolina Board of Public Welfare, had been Nell's primary confidante before she moved to Trenton to become superintendent of the New Jersey State Home for Girls. Impulsively, Nell retrieved Kate's work telephone number from her address book and placed a long distance call with the operator, hoping Kate might still be in her office. After only two rings, to her great relief she heard Kate's voice. "I hate to bother you at the end of a busy day," said Nell, "but I'm here in my new law office, you received the announcement, I'm sure. Yes, yes, just down from the Capitol, I'm still getting settled in. I'm in a quandary over whether to accept a case which will be my first and promises to be difficult. It could make me or break me."

Kate interrupted her. "Of course you'll represent those firebugs," she said. "I've heard all about it. News travels fast through the reform school grapevine, and I still read the Raleigh paper, especially your Sunday column. You can take the girl out of Carolina, but you can't take Carolina out of the girl. You also can't take the crusader out of Battling Nell."

"I'd be going against many of our friends in the women's clubs," said Nell. "They won't like it when I attack the very institution we worked so hard to establish. And I'll be contradicting my own endorsement of Miss MacNaughton."

"Agnes MacNaughton seems to have lost her marbles," said Kate. "She's labored too long in the fields of the Lord."

67

Nell replied, "Perhaps I should have perceived her feet of clay much sooner. She always seemed a bit peculiar, her devotion to that dog of hers, what's his name, Jack, treats him like a king. And so close to that decidedly unattractive Miss Crenshaw she hired as discipline officer. You know Claire Crenshaw has been an animal trainer for a circus?"

"Live and learn," said Kate. "This is a capital case. The lives of those girls are in jeopardy. George McNeill in Carthage may have been appointed to represent them, but you'd be doing the lion's share of the work. A little bird told me David Sinclair down in Wilmington has been asked to represent the Pridgen girl, but he doesn't want to touch this case with a ten-foot pole. Typical male lawyer, real Southern gentleman, doesn't care about the rights of poor girls who've been branded with the scarlet letter. That's why we need more female attorneys in the Tar Heel State. You have a calling, my dear."

The news that David Sinclair intended to reject Margaret Pridgen as a client pushed a button inside Nell. "As always, Kate, you've given me clarity. I'll keep you posted on what happens, and it's happening fast."

"You focus on defending those girls with the truth of their circumstances at Samarcand," said Kate, "and the devil take the hindmost. I'll read about you in the newspapers. Story's spreading far and wide."

"Wish I had you here to keep my spirits up," said Nell.

"When you've brought this to a proper conclusion," said Kate, "you can hightail it north for a visit and I'll give you a taste of New Jersey hospitality. We grow blueberries in our pine barrens."

"Done." said Nell. "I'll bring you a basket of Sandhills peaches."

She hung up the telephone and stared at the wall opposite her desk. Perhaps she should add to her office décor the *News and Observer* article announcing her candidacy in 1928 for the North Carolina General Assembly from Wake County. She rummaged in the boxes in the corner of her office and brought forth, somewhat the worse for wear, the framed headline "Well Known Writer and Club Woman Formally Enters June Democratic Primary," mounted over her picture with a bobbed hairdo. She tentatively held the campaign announcement against the wall next to her Loray Mill cartoon. She had lost her bid for public office, though she received more votes than any other Raleigh candidate and made it to the runoff. Kate Burr Johnson had corralled the support of Wake's club women on her behalf, but the mill town of Wake Forest had opposed her candidacy because she championed the cause of labor unions, and Christian fundamentalists conducted a whisper campaign which portrayed her as an atheist. It had been a defeat, but an honorable one, and she was glad she had made the effort. Now she took the hammer and a new nail and resolutely affixed to the wall the relic of her political adventure.

While she was at it, she also put on display a banner promoting Democratic New York Governor Al Smith's 1928 Presidential candidacy. Smith was Roman Catholic, anathema in the South, which whetted Nell's appetite to make campaign stump speeches for him. As governor, he had implemented a Child Welfare Act to award pensions to widows with children, and he battled against corporate interests. Nell believed that opposition against Smith in North Carolina was fuelled by Duke Power and Carolina Power & Light companies. When Herbert

Hoover won in a landslide, Nell wrote in her column that religious prejudice against Smith was a violation of the principles of American democracy and of Jesus Christ. "Glory to the Protestant god in the highest," she said, "in the United States intolerance and ill-will toward Roman Catholics." She realized she risked losing potential clients who might take offense at her Al Smith for President banner, but it was her law office and she did not intend to kow-tow to those who sought her services. Because of her reputation for championing the cause of the little people, she doubted whether many corporate clients would be coming her way.

Still procrastinating about writing her letter regarding the Samarcand defendants, she labelled the drawers of her file cabinets "Active," "Inactive," "Personal," and "Nell Battle Lewis, Attorney at Law." Into the latter she placed file folders marked "North Carolina Bar," "Taxes," "Utilities," "Supplies," "Clerical." She had no inactive cases, and her only active case would be the Samarcand arson defendants, so that drawer was yet to be filled. Into the "Personal" drawer she placed behind the letter "B" correspondence from her brothers Kemp, Ivey, and Dick; behind the letter "C" she placed matters pertaining to Lenoir Chambers and correspondence with Episcopal Bishop Joseph Cheshire; "D" would hold correspondence with Josephus and Jonathan Daniels, and "P" poems by NBL. Changing her mind, she quickly removed the folder for Lenoir Chambers, wryly thinking it should more appropriately be placed in the "Inactive" drawer. Then she realized she did not want anyone, including a future office assistant, to be privy to what had transpired between Lewis and Chambers, and she would be better served keeping any mementoes of their relationship in a locked drawer of her bedroom dresser at home. They had no place in her law office.

She slammed all the file drawers shut. Patience with maintenance was not her forte. Perhaps with the small fee she obtained for defending the Samarcand sixteen, she might hire a part-time clerk to put her files in order. Now, with twilight falling, she would make a commitment to take on this task. She again opened the "Nell Battle Lewis, Attorney at Law" drawer and removed two sheets of stationery and placed them into her typewriter, along with a sheet of carbon paper. Dating her letter March 25, 1931, she began:

Dear Mrs. Williams,

I am in receipt of your request that I represent the defendants charged with arson in the burning of two buildings at Samarcand Manor, and I accept your offer of a nominal fee for my services.

I shall immediately begin to investigate, as time is of the essence and this is a complex matter involving so many clients. I will do my best on their behalf and shall keep you informed of my progress.

Sincerely,

Nell Battle Lewis

c/o U. S. Post Office Fayetteville Street

Raleigh, North Carolina

Nell filed the carbon copy of her letter into a folder marked "Samarcand," along with the letter from Mrs. Williams and the statement of Miss Viola Sistare. And so it begins, she thought, as she licked a two-cent stamp and placed it in the upper righthand corner of an envelope she addressed to Mrs. Williams. She turned off her desk lamp and exited her office. The hallway was empty; indeed the entire building seemed empty, for it was late in the day, banking hours were over, and most occupants were well on their way home for supper.

Crossing Fayetteville Street, she realized the post office also would be closed, so she mailed her letter in the box on the corner, which stated pickup would occur at nine in the morning. She felt exhausted, wanting to turn her mind to something other than the plight of the Samarcand arsonists, whom she would soon meet in person. Walking to the Christ Church parking lot where she kept her car, she shivered slightly in the evening chill. She thought perhaps she should start taking the trolley downtown, rather than parking her car at the church where she had serious differences with the rector. But that was a decision to make tomorrow or the day after; she had made enough decisions today.

Now she would drive to her house on St. Mary's Street, where she would content herself with a glass or two of sherry along with cheddar cheese, beaten biscuits, and a tin of canned ham as she listened to radio station WPTF to catch news of the Scottsboro incident involving nine Negroes and two white women. If the men alleged to have committed rape managed to avoid lynching, their fate in an Alabama court would likely not be a tribute to American justice. And it would be largely up to Nell to seek and find true justice for her sixteen wayward white girls in North Carolina; this would require every ounce of energy she could muster, and no doubt the path would not be smooth.

3

The Interrogations

With the trial set for May 19, less than a month away, Nell knew she had no time to waste if she were to mount a credible defense for the Samarcand girls. She felt the enormity of the case bearing down upon her, at times seeming to suffocate and induce a sense of helplessness. She dreamed she was in a strange city and had lost her car, or she was walking in public in the nude, and she knew these to be subconscious manifestations of anxiety. Self-doubt was her constant companion. Was her training adequate? After all, she had only read law, not graduated from law school. Would her lack of prior courtroom experience be too great a handicap? Her zeal, her passion, was well established, but she wished she had the same faith in her trial abilities as did those who urged her to take the case. Yet taken it she had, and lives were at stake; the girls were depending upon her. She must enter the courtroom fully prepared, with every scrap of information she could muster, every argument she hoped to make fully substantiated. There could be no room for error.

During her adult life she had championed the cause of the state's poor, the down and out, the dispossessed, especially girls

73

and women. She entertained no illusion the state's legal system had the defendants' best interests at heart. She had seen North Carolina's legal system at work with the Gastonia mill strikers, and she knew it had little regard for justice or even rudimentary fairness. The hopes of Margaret Pridgen's family, which had played such a prominent role in her decision to take the case, were similar to those of the families of the other defendants, and these families with few resources were counting on her not to disappoint. This case, she felt, would be hers to win or lose, although she hoped she could work cooperatively with George McNeill, whom she looked forward to meeting. But for the moment she was on her own, and she had never felt so alone. For an instant she was tempted to call Lenoir Chambers at his new workplace, the Norfolk *Virginian Pilot,* for advice on how best to approach the trial, but quickly realized how foolish she might seem, and how weak.

The girls held the key to a successful defense. While others could corroborate their stories, it would be the girls themselves who would have to convince the court they had acted for cause, that the Samarcand arson was not merely a spiteful act of violence and vengeance. Nell knew a proper defense would be impossible unless she heard their stories, sat and talked with each girl, looked into her eyes and watched the expressions on her face as she answered Nell's questions. Why they had been sent to Samarcand she could learn from other sources, but what had happened to them there, the experiences which transformed them from hapless girls into angry young women desperate enough to attempt to burn the place to the ground, only they could tell, and their accounts would lie at the heart of her defense.

Carthage

Before starting her trip to Carthage, Nell drove by North Carolina's Central Prison, which stood only minutes from her home. She needed to look the devil in the eye, she told herself, face down her fears. The main building, a square six-story tower, was built in 1884 of granite quarried near the site. A series of turrets housing guards armed with machine guns topped the structure. Nell thought it hideously ugly, almost evil, an admission of humanity's dark side and society's failure to control it. Why, she wondered, had Raleigh's leaders sited the prison in their city, North Carolina's capital, what message had they thought its presence sent the state's citizens? Had such thoughts crossed their minds? Or had they thought of the construction jobs it would bring, the staff it would hire, and purchases of supplies, equipment and services it would make? Somewhere inside, she knew, sat what the press corps had dubbed "Old Sparky," an overlarge wooden chair with leather straps and electrodes which was the state's official instrument of death. She hated the death penalty, time and again had denounced it in her columns as arbitrary, inhumane, and barbaric, a position that inevitably resulted in readers' letters recommending the chair for her. She took a last look, vowed to see that the Samarcand girls never met Old Sparky, and do her utmost to prevent them from ever stepping inside Central Prison.

On this pleasant late-April day she quickly left Raleigh behind and found herself enjoying the two-hour trip. Most of the travel was along U. S. Highway 1, a two-lane concrete ribbon running from Maine to Florida, slicing through central North Carolina and its sandhills. She passed tobacco fields with rows

75

of recently transplanted seedlings which would be ready for harvest by July, fields cleared for planting the next corn crop, and gardens with beans and peas and turnips. She passed pine forests, stands of sweetgum and oak, flowering white dogwoods and redbuds, their color just beginning to show, and forests entwined with the vines of flowering jessamine, its luster of bright yellow visible in the distance. She could almost forget that people who tended the farms and fields and ran the stores and businesses of the agricultural communities dotting the highway remained in the grip of the Depression, struggling to support families. The road took her through hamlets with general stores, selling whatever customers needed, from bread to buttons, shoes to sausage. Some had large metal signs mounted high above the ground on painted steel poles, announcing a brand of gasoline, Gulf, Esso, Shell, Mobil. Larger communities, like Cary and Apex, boasted department and dime stores, tourist homes, agricultural implement dealerships, a hotel or two. Sanford, with its small downtown shopping district, was the only place where she encountered traffic and multiple stop lights, causing her repeatedly to hit her brakes and shift gears. Arriving in Carthage, Nell easily found a convenient parking space.

Sheriff McDonald met her as soon as she came through the door, hand extended. "Pleased to meet you, Miss Battle," he said. Still fit, his dark hair graying at the temples, he wore the sheriff's uniform. "I appreciate your call and have been looking forward to your visit. We've things all arranged for you to speak with our rather unusual guests."

"Thank you," Nell replied. "Can't say I've look forward to this visit, but I appreciate your cooperation."

"No trouble. We have a small interrogation room all prepared. If there's anything else you require, you have only to ask."

"I think I have all I need. I'd like to carry my brief case with me for the interviews; it holds my notepads and pencils. I hope this is acceptable?"

"Certainly, no problem. Let the guard know when you've finished an interview, who you'd like to see next." The sheriff motioned to a uniformed figure in the hallway. "The guard should have them down within minutes. A pleasure to meet you, Miss Battle. I've read a number of your columns in the Raleigh paper." He turned. "John, please take Miss Lewis to the interrogation room, see she's comfortable, and bring her the Samarcand girls as she requests them. One at a time, please." Nell followed the guard into a small room furnished only with two chairs and small table.

"Which girl would you like to speak with first, Miss Battle?" the guard asked.

Nell had already formed an answer. "Please bring Margaret Pridgen." The guard soon ushered into the room a slight girl with a distinctive nose and brown hair. Her facial expression was a mixture of fear and curiosity, her body language suggesting resignation to whatever she must endure. "Hello, Margaret," Nell said. "I'm Nell Lewis, and I am going to be your attorney."

"A lady lawyer? I didn't know they had lady lawyers." Margaret moved further into the room.

"There aren't many, it's true," Nell said. "But I am one, and I'm going to help you. First I need you to answer a few

77

questions. You can do that for me, can't you?" Margaret nodded yes. "Take a seat at the table, please." Nell began the series of questions she had prepared for each of the girls, while trying to put Margaret at ease. "Tell me a bit about your family, your mother and father, if you have any brothers and sisters."

"My daddy is Strange Pridgen. That's his real name, Strange. He's a carpenter. And my mother's name is Edell. That's Edell with two e's and two l's. She stays home. I have two brothers and three sisters."

"And they live in Wilmington?"

"Yes, ma'm."

"Do you miss home, Margaret?"

"Very much. I been here too long."

"Did you go to school in Wilmington?"

"Yes, ma'm. Started when I was about seven and went pretty regular. Finished the fourth grade before they sent me away. I liked school. I like to study words."

"Do you know why you came to Samarcand, Margaret?"

"I didn't come. They sent me. Told me it was for being mean and running around."

"Did you run around?"

"Sometimes I would be with boys, but I didn't do nothing wrong, except maybe smoke a cigarette. My daddy didn't want me with my friends, though. He wanted me always near to home, helping with my brothers. Sometimes I just wanted to have a little fun. But Daddy's church didn't want girls to have fun. They did let us smoke cigarettes, though."

78

"Now, Margaret, I want to ask you a very important question, and I want you to answer me honestly. Did you ever mess around with any of these boys? You know what I mean."

Margaret hesitated. "No, ma'm, not til I was thirteen. Then just one time, with this boy, my cousin. We went to the beach in his car, stayed out late. That's why my daddy had me sent to Samarcand, I reckon. They told me I'm not supposed to talk about what happened in my life before I got here. But I reckon it's all right to talk about it to you."

For an instant, Nell relived the hurt and anger she herself had felt more than a decade earlier, when her own father sabotaged her engagement to Lenoir Chambers. She empathized with Margaret's feelings of helplessness when faced with her father's interference. Startled by her emotional response to Margaret's answer, Nell abandoned the subject of boys, moving quickly to a less problematic topic which, considering the arson, was redundant but had to be documented in preparation for the trial. "Then let's talk about Samarcand. How do you like it?"

"I hate it. It's an awful place," Margaret's voice rose in anger.

The vehemence of her response took Nell by surprise. "Why do you say that?"

"Some of the teachers treat you so mean. They don't mind cursing you. The two Shaws, Miz Crenshaw and Miz Bradshaw, they are the meanest. They whip us, beat us with heavy sticks, sometimes with leather belts. Miz MacNaughton holds the girls while the teachers beat us."

"Have you ever been whipped, Margaret?"

"Yes, ma'm. Once."

79

"Do you know why you were whipped?"

"Yes, ma'm. Leastways I know what Miz MacNaughton said. She said it was because I tried to run away and I carried some dessert to a girl locked in the discipline room. She was hungry,"

Again Margaret's response surprised Nell. "The discipline room?"

"Yes, ma'm. That's where they put you if you are bad or uppity or rude."

"I want you to tell me about the night of the fire at Samarcand. I've heard you set a fire. If this is true, I need to know."

"Yes, ma'm. I don't know nothing about the fire in Bickett, but that night when I saw it burning I made up my mind to burn Chamberlain. Lots of girls in Chamberlain started talking about burning it down, but it was me that lit the fire. I shouldn't have been in Chamberlain, didn't want to be there. Wanted to go to an honor cottage if I couldn't go home."

Margaret looked hard at Nell. "You really a lawyer? I guess you know a lot of words."

Nell smiled. "It's using the right words that counts, Margaret, and how you use them."

"Could I be a lady lawyer like you? I would like that. I don't want to be a carpenter like my father. And my mother, she's not really anything. She just has babies."

"Oh, Margaret," replied Nell, "babies are interesting. You could be a lawyer AND have babies." As she spoke, Nell realized that few of the women professionals she knew had children.

"Do you have babies?" asked Margaret.

Nell felt a slight pang and evaded this question. "Right now, we must tend to your situation with Samarcand."

"Sure," said Margaret, "I was looking at a whipping the next day. So I thought maybe if I started a fire, they would send me home. I went to my room, to the closet. There was a paper dress hanging in there, and I lit it on fire. Then I shut the door to make sure it would burn, that nobody could put it out, and I just stood there 'til I could see it was good and on fire." She related her central role in the Samarcand fires as calmly as if she were describing what she had for supper. Nell was amazed by how easily she told the story, with a degree of pride and without the slightest hint of remorse.

"Did you talk with Miss MacNaughton about this the night of the fire?"

"Oh, yes, ma'm."

"Were you alone when you talked, just you and Miss MacNaughton?"

"No, ma'm. Miz Stott was there, too."

"No other girls?"

"Just me."

"Did you tell Miss MacNaughton you set the fire?"

"I told her right off I done it. She said I might have to go to jail. I never expected that. I thought they would send me home. Been a long time since I've been home." Margaret paused for a moment, gazing toward the window as she attempted to control a quiver of her lips. "I really miss my family, especially my, umm, baby sister. She just got born before they sent me away. But I

81

guess you know that. I'm not supposed to talk about it. They tell you at Samarcand, you can't say anything about your life before you came there, you have to forget all what happened before." Margaret looked earnestly at Nell. "But I can't forget my life I had. Can you?"

Nell put down her pen and pinched the bridge of her nose to force back tears as she looked at the girl who sat with her arms folded protectively against her body, slowly rocking to and fro, as if she were holding an infant. "Thank you, Margaret, you've been very cooperative," said Nell. "I promise I'm going to help you all I can. I'll let your family know I'm helping, and I think you're a good girl."

As Margaret stood to leave, Nell had a sudden, disconcerting thought. Her father had staunchly supported the State's eugenics program, which was carried out by forced sterilizations of girls like Margaret. When Nell protested the state had no right to sterilize women without their consent, contending the program was immoral at a fundamental level, her father brushed aside her objections. Kept the feebleminded and insane from breeding, he said, otherwise they would multiply like rabbits, drag down the entire race. All advanced European nations, especially Britain and Germany, had eugenics movements supported by prominent men she admired, he reminded her, such men as George Bernard Shaw, H.G. Wells, and Winston Churchill. With its recent wave of immigrants, America, he maintained, was even more in need of an effective eugenics program to insure that the best elements of society would not be overwhelmed.

Dreading the answer she might receive, Nell asked, "Did you ever have appendicitis, Margaret?"

Margaret appeared surprised by the question. A puzzled look on her face, she placed her hand on her abdomen. "Yes, ma'm, I did."

Saddened by Margaret's response, Nell watched the girl leave the room, affected by her almost childlike innocence. Something in the way she spoke about her baby sister raised a question in Nell's mind, and she wrote a note to check the date of the sister's birth and compare this with Margaret's banishment from Wilmington. She also made a note to request that Margaret be examined by a psychologist. She would, she suspected, make such a request for others of the sixteen.

None of the other six girls was as forthcoming as Margaret, and although all revealed a similar naiveté, they lacked Margaret's quality of innocence. Virginia Hayes denied she had any part in the Samarcand fires, yet admitted she had said she participated. "Miz MacNaughton made me say I was in it. I said, 'Well, if I've got the name to bear, you can think what you please.' I wanted to go home because I had just got a letter saying my mother was sick, but Miz MacNaughton wouldn't let me see my mother or go home to help out my brothers. She said I shou'n't have run away from home, which is what got me to Samarcand, and since I did, I would have to lie in my bed there, since I helped make it." A brief smile flashed across Virginia's face. "Who wants to lie in a bed which has bedbugs?"

Nell found the girl's confession entirely reasonable from the perspective of a fifteen-year-old with a sixth-grade education who had been committed to Samarcand, and she nodded her head at the mention of bedbugs. "I was in that bed when the second fire in Chamberlain started," Virginia continued. "The attendant, Miz Ross, she wouldn't open the doors of our rooms so we could get out, but she gave some of the girls her keys."

"You mean you girls had to let yourselves out of your rooms?" Nell asked incredulously.

"I expect Miz Ross was afraid of the fire." Yes, Nell thought, I expect she was.

Spontaneously, Nell asked, "How is your health, Virginia?"

Virginia appeared pleased Nell cared to ask this personal question. "I had pneumonia three times," she answered. "And I had the scarlet fever. My mother, she's right sickly, I guess I got her blood."

"Did you ever have appendicitis?"

Virginia gently put her hand on her belly. "They took my appendix out two weeks ago at Moore hospital. Sent me over when I was in the jail, said it would help me with the cramps when, you know, I have my monthly. But I hadn't noticed no cramps problem. I was in the hospital five days. I'm still kind of sore."

Nell nodded sympathetically, disguising a sudden flash of anger on behalf of this unsuspecting girl. "I hope you feel better soon, Virginia," she said.

Marian Mercer had an interesting appearance, high cheekbones, dark hair, a bronze cast to her skin. She leaned forward and cocked her head when Nell spoke, fixing her gaze on Nell's lips. "Do you have a problem with your hearing?" Nell asked.

"I'm deaf," the girl answered matter-of-factly in a voice somewhat monotone, with unusual pronunciation of words. "But not total deaf. I can hear if you speak slow and I try real hard to un'erstand. My name is really Mary Susan, but sometime folks started calling me Marian, so that is fine with me."

"All right," Nell continued, "please tell me about your family, life back home."

"My daddy was a sailor, but he drowned. I can't hardly remember nothing about him, except his boots, he wore big rubber boots. And I remember sometimes he smelt of fish."

"And your mother?"Nell asked.

"They say my real mother died when I was four. Her name was Rosetta, and they say she was Indian and I look like her. Then I lived with my g'anmother til I was put in the county home. Then I was sent to stay with Miss Dicie Page in Ayden, and stayed wif her until I was thirteen. Her hu'band worked in a saw mill. I liked the way he smelt, like pine trees."

Nell realized the girl's story about her mother's death was not true, likely a myth she had been told. According to Samarcand admission records stated, Rosetta had run a brothel after her husband's death, had remarried, and had several other children. ike so many of the other girls, Marian had been labelled promiscuous and shipped off to Samarcand, although she vehemently denied the charge.

Nell found Mary Susan-Marian only slightly less naive than Margaret. She freely admitted helping to start the fires and seemed to take some pride in doing so.. "Me and Peg Abernethy set Chamberlain on fire the first time. Me and her went back in the kitchen and got some matches, and we lit a stocking in the attic. I thought that would get me home."

"Did you tell Miss MacNaughton this?" Nell asked, enunciating crisply. She anticipated Marian's answer. There

85

was nothing which would cause a fifteen-year-old girl with less than a sixth-grade education to be circumspect in speaking with Miss MacNaughton, especially when it was an effort for her to communicate at all.

"Yes, ma'm, I told Miz M'Naugh'on," Marian replied, seemingly still oblivious to the import of her response.

Nell made a note to have her examined by a psychologist. She found the girls' lives before Samarcand, and the reasons for their commitment, sadly similar. Rosa Mull, a thirteen-year-old from the mountain town of Rutherfordton, came from a poor family of four children with a mother hospitalized for pellagra, and said she was sent to Samarcand for running away from home. Josephine French, a fifteen-year-old hosiery mill worker from Haw River, said she and her mother were deserted by her father when she was two years old. She followed her mother into the mill while still a child. A welfare officer sent her to Samarcand because she had been running around with boys. "At Samarcand, they beat us with great big sticks," said Josephine. "I was locked in my room with the bedbugs for a month because I tried to run away." She asked Nell, "Wouldn't you want to run away from beatings and bedbugs?" Nell resisted the urge to nod in the affirmative, not wanting it to be said she approved of the girls' fiery rebellion, although she was fully sympathetic.

Another mountain girl, Wilma Owens of Waynesville, said she lost her mother to pellagra. "Mama didn't get enough to eat," said Wilma. "She gave most all the food to us. She didn't have hardly nothing, and she got sick." She added, "My daddy killed hisself right in front of me. I thought it was my fault, because I couldn't take care of things good as Mama did, and Daddy was so tired and feeling so sad. They sent my brother and three sisters to an orphanage in Thomasville, but I didn't want to go, so I went to live with a cousin who acted like she would be good to me. But she fooled me. She wanted me to, you know, be with men for money, like she was doing. I didn't want to, and she got me took to jail on a bunch of lies. From jail I got took to Samarcand. After that, they let me out for awhile, then I got took to Samarcand again." Wilma's face assumed a quizzical expression. "You know what I think, Miz Lewis? I think some of them sheriff deputies used to stop in at my cousin's place. And they didn't have to pay her nothing. That's what I think, because they didn't put my cousin in jail, they put me in jail because I wouldn't do nothing with them."

Nell felt fairly certain Wilma was correct in what she thought, and she asked a follow-up question. "Did you ever have an operation for appendicitis?"

"I sure did," said Wilma. "Up to the hospital at Waynesville, between the two times I was at Samarcand. The operation hurt, but I got along real good with the nurses, and they liked me. I thought maybe I could do nursing, too."

To Nell's dismay, Thelma Council, the daughter of a tenant farmer, who lost her mother as a child, responded positively to the question about appendicitis. "Yes, ma'm. They took it out right after I got here to the Lumberton jail." Three of the girls Nell interviewed had been operated on for appendicitis, and a fourth may have been scheduled, under the auspices of the State, not as children, when appendicitis usually strikes, but as adolescents assumed to be sexually active. Surely this could not be coincidental. Wilma and Margaret and Virginia and Rosa and Marian were the kind of girls, poor, uneducated, lacking family support, for whom Nell had once hoped Samarcand would provide a refuge.

She had believed Samarcand could transform girls like this into legitimately self-supporting women who contributed constructively to society, with families of their own which had more security than they themselves had experienced in their young lives. This was why she had helped the campaign to establish Samarcand, why she had served for years on the state board which oversaw its direction, why she had used her newspaper column to persuade the public that Samarcand could help rehabilitate the shattered lives of youth living at the frayed edges of society. Samarcand was part of her mission, her secular crusade to save the lost, especially women and children who lacked the power to protect themselves.

But the fires had exposed the rot in the marrow of Samarcand. Beneath the pleasing outward appearance of the reform school set in the tall pines and bucolic farmland, with the idyllic chapel for worship and the well-organized performances put on for visitors, festered physical and emotional abuse which sabotaged Samarcand's stated purpose. The superintendent's own demons had been at work, permitting and perhaps enjoying the sadism which further victimized victims entrusted to her care. The girls' descriptions of life at Samarcand, their depressingly similar tales of constant disparagement and continuing abuse, made Nell sick at heart, especially when she realized she had unknowingly enabled the situation to exist. Most shocking to her were the girls' matter-of-fact responses to her queries about punishment, as if such heinous treatment was to be endured until it became a pot which boiled over. Perhaps this was because they had suffered so much abuse before they arrived at Samarcand that they assumed it to be the norm. They must have believed that the authorities who oversaw

Samarcand's operations knew about and approved the abuse as part of the girls' rehabilitation.

The girls' answers and their long-smoldering anger, at last bursting into flame, left no room for rebuttal. Rosa Mull detested Samarcand, tried to run away three times and had been beaten. Josephine French was beaten twice, "with great big sticks" and locked in her room for a month for attempting to run away. Marian Mercer said she "hated Samarcand." So did Virginia Hayes, who neatly summed up the experiences and attitudes of all seven girls: "They just treat you terrible, give horse whippings, make you fire up the furnace, make you sleep on one blanket on the floor, better be anywhere than be in Samarcand." How ironic, Nell thought, that she herself might help Virginia Hayes get her wish to be anywhere else. If she lost the case, Virginia might soon be released from Samarcand, from jail, and from this world entirely because she had participated in committing a death penalty offense. Yet Nell detected nothing in the demeanor of the girls to indicate they were aware they faced the possibility of execution. She sighed, remembering her own youth. Young people magically believe they will live forever, that they are exempt from the mortality which prematurely took their mothers, as it had taken Nell's own mother so many years before, when she herself was a little girl.

After the last girl left the interview room, Nell sat briefly reviewing her notes. She allowed herself to entertain the idea that the girls could be lying, at least be guilty of exaggeration. They had lived together since the fires, with plenty of time and nothing else to do but coordinate their stories. The seven girls jailed at Carthage obviously were considered to be the most incorrigible of the Samarcand Sixteen. They were in Carthage jail, after all, because they had set fire to the Lumberton jail, and at least three admitted to setting the conflagration at Samarcand. But listening to and observing them, she found them to be fully credible, without guile.

Leaving the jail, Nell walked to the nearby office of George McNeil, whom she had yet to meet. She hoped to discuss the case with him, but was disappointed to find him not in. She collected a notepad from her purse and wrote a brief message:

Dear Mr. McNeil,

I am sorry to have missed you, as I had hoped we could discuss cooperating on the defense of the Samarcand girls, as I am aware of your connection to the case. At the request of some women concerned about the girls, I have agreed to represent them. I am sure that you agree that these unfortunate girls should have their case presented as effectively as possible, and I hope that you will give me the benefit of your ability and experience to that end, and that I shall have the honor of being associated with you in their defense. I expect to return to Carthage in the near future and hope we can meet at that time. In the meantime, please do not hesitate to contact me by letter or phone. I am attaching my card for your convenience.

Sincerely,

Nell Battle Lewis

Clipping her card to the note, she slipped them beneath the door.

George McNeil found her note the next morning and could hardly believe his good fortune. He could use all the help he could get, but the prospect of working with Nell Battle Lewis seemed too good to be true. Not only would he gain a female attorney for the defense, he would be working with one of the best-known personalities in the state, a woman with ties to

Raleigh's leading families, and with a professional and personal relationship with the publisher of the state's leading newspaper. Whatever the outcome of the case, working with Nell Lewis would mean unprecedented exposure for him. Moving to his desk, he composed an immediate reply. He would, he assured her, be delighted to assist her in the defense of the girls, even if the trial judge chose not to appoint him to continue to work for those girls not financially able to retain an attorney, and he looked forward to conferring with her the next time she came to town.

Four days after her visit to Carthage, and a day after receiving George McNeil's offer of cooperation, Nell took her second road trip from Raleigh, this time down Highway 301 to Lumberton, the county seat of Robeson County, to question the remaining Samarcand defendants. She held a faint hope the Lumberton girls would tell less horrific stories than had those in Carthage, and restore some of her initial faith in Samarcand. George McNeil's response had also buoyed her confidence together they could mount a winning defense, if not for all, at least for a large majority of the defendants, and that the death penalty could be avoided even if a small number were convicted.

Entering Robeson County, one of the state's poorest regions, Nell reflected on its population, a unique, equal mixture of whites, mostly of Scottish descent, blacks, and Lumbee Indians. The Lumbee, like the town, took their name from the Lumber River, upon whose banks the town was situated. Except for the Cherokee in the western part of North Carolina, the Lumbee were the largest Native American tribe east of the Mississippi River, though not officially recognized by the federal government. They had adapted to the ways of the white settlers, retreated to swamps and byways, and eked out a livelihood on small farms and as tradesmen, often hiring out their services to their white neighbors.

In 1888 the state had established a normal school at Pembroke, a village just west of Lumberton, to supply teachers for the segregated society's third public school system. This system was necessary because brown-skinned Lumbees considered themselves superior to black-skinned citizens, and though legally banned from white schools, refused to attend schools for blacks. Poverty, the dynamics of racial segregation, and a shared cultural trait of settling grievances personally rather than through the legal system each group mistrusted, meant that Robeson County experienced more than its share of violence, even for a Southern community, and its jail was often full. The Lumberton jail was not a place one would want a daughter housed, even temporarily. Arriving at the jail a block from the courthouse, Nell was met by chief jailer Austin Smith.

"We're ready for you, Miss Lewis," he said. "The girls get bored in their cells, always glad to have company."

"Do they get many visitors?"

"A couple days after they got here some of the ladies from the Lumberton Women's Club come to see them. Brought a bunch of stuff, clothes, hair brushes, combs, tooth brushes and tooth paste, things like that. Thank God they brought the clothes, 'cause what them girls had on when they got here, it was next to nothing, really, and what they had was mostly rags."

Nell was touched by Smith's obvious concern for the girls. "And did the ladies return?"

"A couple more times, and brought more stuff. The girls really appreciated it. Since then, ain't been many visitors, not even family. One or two reporters. 'Course, it's been a sight quieter since they took them other girls back to Carthage." He motioned toward a doorway. "You can do your questioning in there, have your privacy. I'll see you ain't interrupted. Tell me who all you need."

"I'd like to start with Margaret Abernethy, please."

"That girl is a strange one, Miss Lewis," Smith replied. "I sort of feel sorry for her. I'll have her here in a minute."

Nell saw a small, thin, wisp of a girl with blond hair and bad complexion enter the room. She felt a surge of sympathy for the timid sixteen-year-old, before she found out why the jailer called this a strange one. "Hello, Margaret," Nell said. "I'm Nell Lewis, your attorney, and I'd like to ask you a few questions. Please have a seat." Margaret sat without speaking. "Tell me something about yourself. Where are you from?"

"I used to live in Kinston," Margaret replied haltingly. "I like to be called Peg. The girls all call me that."

"Okay, Peg. Did you live with your family?"

The girl cleared her throat as she looked away from Nell. "With my daddy. I don't remember my real mother. They told me she died. Willie Green was my other mother, she raised me. She weren't kind to me at all."

"Do you have brothers or sisters?"

"After she come to live with us my other mother had a boy and a girl. She just had the girl when I come to Samarcand."

Nell sensed a pattern emerging regarding the girls' commitment to reform school, new babies in their households. "And your father?"

Peg's entire body stiffened, but her voice betrayed no emotion as she answered the question. "He's in prison. They sent him to prison for forcing me."

"Forcing you?" Nell tried not to show her shock.

"Yes, ma'm." Peg looked down at the floor. "When my other mother would leave the house, when my daddy was drunk. But not every time."

Nell felt anger again rise inside her, on behalf of this girl. "Tell me, how old were you when the forcing started?" She struggled to maintain composure.

"When I was about ten, I reckon. I didn't want it. Didn't know what it was at first. And I didn't like how he smelt, likkered up. He kept me scared. Said he'd kill me sure if I tolt anyone. My other mother didn't know nothing about it until the end. She was busy with the baby while my daddy slipped down to my room. But then she caught him doing it. After she found out, my daddy, his name was Ivey, he said he was going to kill me, it was my fault, I tempted him.

"He talked about the Bible, how Eve tempted Adam, made him sin against God. So I ran away to a lady's house not far off. She got the police and they carried my daddy off to jail. They took me to the county home, but I didn't like it and I run away. Then I lived with a woman who kept children for the welfare. When the law sent my daddy to Central Prison up at Raleigh, they sent me to Samarcand. I don't hardly reckon that was fair, to send me away. I didn't do nothing. I was forced. And it hurt me when he did it to me, got me so I could hardly sit down.

"Why would I want to do that with my own daddy?," asked Peg. "I sure never run around with boys. He wouldn't let me, wanted to keep me for his own self. And I sure didn't want to do that thing with anybody else. I used to try to hide where my daddy wouldn't find me. I looked away from boys when they got near me. I just wanted to be left alone."

I guess you did want to be left alone, Nell thought, to be able to live like the child you were, without anybody putting his hands on you. She did her best to suppress rising anger as she thought, no, it wasn't fair, not at all, and here you are through no fault of your own, and only God knows what will happen next. Nell ruminated. What was wrong with so many men? Why did they violate their own flesh and blood? Were they so selfish, so lacking in respect for their daughters and wives? Men like that should be castrated as punishment for such violation, rather than society's performing "Mississippi appendectomies" on girls, which would deny them the choice of bearing their own children when they were ready.

She took a deep breath and moved on to another topic. "I understand you've been here for two years, Peg. How do you like Samarcand?"

"It's an awful place. They treat you so mean. I've tried to run away twice."

"How do they treat you mean?"

"They beat us, lock us in our rooms, make us sleep on the floor. And they work us hard, make us do everything, even stoke the furnace."

"Have you been beaten?"

Peg counted off on the fingers of one hand. "Four times. They lay you down on a rug on the steps, beat you with straps or big fat switches, sometimes with paddles. They make the other girls watch, when the girls don't want to watch. They beat you hard, especially Miz Stott and Miz Crenshaw do. Sometimes they draw blood. Miz MacNaughton, she likes to hold you down while they beat you. And if you try to run away, they hold you down and cut off all your hair."

96

Good god, thought Nell. These spinsters get some sort of pleasure out of humiliating adolescent girls whom they believe to be sexually promiscuous, inflicting physical pain, sometimes drawing blood, and watching them writhe on the floor in front of other girls. A psychiatrist would have a field day with Samarcand staffers hired to provide a healthy environment to rehabilitate girls who had already been violated, but instead using their charges to relieve their own frustrations. Sado-masochism was alive and well at Samarcand. Margaret was neither lying nor exaggerating. She doubted the girl had the capacity to invent such a story. She sought to restrain outrage as she said, "I understand you weren't happy at Samarcand and wanted to go home. But I need to know if you helped burn the dormitories, and if you told Miss MacNaughton you did." What a passionless response I just made, she thought, but my duty is to prepare for a trial, not rail at those who provoked the rebellion.

"Yes, ma'm, I told her," said Peg. "I didn't have nothing to do with the fire in Bickett, 'cause I was in Chamberlain eating supper when it caught. We decided to set Chamberlain on fire. Ollie Harding went to get the matches, but she never found them, so I did. Then Margaret Pridgen and Marian Mercer went in the attic and lit the fire while I stood watch. But the staff smelt it and put it out, it didn't do no damage. I thought if we set the fire they would send me away, and I was tired of that place, I'd been there more than two year."

"Well, thank you, Peg, for telling me this. I don't have any more questions, so you may go now." Nell made the notation "Request interview by psychologist." With eight more interviews yet to go, Nell silently prayed she would not encounter another tale as poignant as that of Peg Abernathy, for already she was

97

emotionally exhausted. For a moment, Mary Brunson lifted her spirits. A pretty blonde, tall and slender, the sixteen-year-old seemed bright, courteous, and well mannered. During their conversation, Nell caught herself thinking Mary could well have been a student from St. Mary's School in Raleigh if she came from a family with means. Her father, a traveling salesman, and her mother, a bookkeeper, lived with her two sisters in Rocky Mount. They had her committed to Samarcand because she ran off with a girlfriend and a man to Richmond, where she lived for a week in the YWCA.

"I didn't never run around," Mary insisted. "I just had boyfriends, but I never, you know, went all the way with them. I didn't do nothing to be here for."

"You don't like Samarcand?

"No! They make you work too hard, cook, wash, iron, tend crops and animals on the farm. Miz MacNaughton's dog gets treated like a king, while we girls are treated worse than a dog."

"Were you ever punished?"

Mary paused, then answered carefully, as if searching for just the right words. "No, I never was punished, not beat or anything, except being sent to Chamberlain for being rude to a teacher."

"And did you help set the fire, or tell Miss MacNaughton you did?"

"I told her I heard some girls say they were going to burn Chamberlain down, but I didn't know who did it, except Margaret Pridgen. Marian Mercer said I did it, but that was a lie. I didn't. I didn't confess to it, neither, not to Miz MacNaughton, not to anybody."

Nell was relieved that Mary's story was less salacious than those of the other girls. The other seven defendants provided little which wasn't a repetition of what she had heard from the Carthage girls, Peg Abernethy and Mary Brunson. Though backgrounds varied as to some details, all the girls had been committed for violating prevailing sexual mores, or the suspicion they might violate them, or for being the victim of someone who sexually violated them, which was interpreted as somehow being the girl's fault.

Edna Clark, a pretty, spirited brunette, polite and curious, had living parents who sent her to Samarcand for not attending school and "going with boys." Others, like eighteen- year-old Bertha Hall, had lost both parents. Married at fifteen to her sixteen-year-old cousin and becoming a mother less than a year later, she was committed by her husband when she accused him of being unfaithful. When seventeen-year-old Ollie Harding lost her mother, her father "was mean to her," so she ran away to have a life of her own. In retaliation, her father had her sent to Samarcand. What they all reported, Nell was not surprised to hear, was that Samarcand was a horror show.

"They didn't treat me right. They would beat me and lock me up," said Ollie Harding.

Pearl Stiles watched "girls whipped so sometimes they would put water in their faces to keep them from fainting, so they could keep beating on them. " She said she was beaten once.

Edna Clark said she was beaten three times, once so severely "I had to be taken to the hospital and painted." The hospital, Nell knew, was on campus, and she assumed Edna had the cuts from her beating treated with iodine, which would feel like pouring salt in the wounds.

Estelle Wilson, though never beaten, said, "They were too mean to you—they would lock me up every time I turned around."

Ollie Harding told Nell she was "beaten with hickories" for trying to slip in a letter. "The teacher held my head. Miz Ross, Miz Crenshaw, and Miz MacNaughton all helped beat me." The girls' litany of abuse prompted Nell to ask if any of the Samarcand staff had treated them well. Once again, each girl responded with a similar answer, one which surprised her.

According to Bertha Hall, "The two Northern teachers were more friendly to us and treated us more decently."

Ollie Harding said of these women, "They was good to me. Seems like they wuz kinder free-hearted and had feelings for us girls."

Estelle Wilson replied the Northern teachers "seemed to have more feeling" and "I loved Miz Sistare."

Edna Clark added a poignant twist to her response that she liked the two Northern teachers "pretty well," when she said Miss MacNaughton "was good to me except when she beat me." This comment rang in Nell's ears, that Miss Mac was good except when she was bad, nice except when she was mean. A typical reaction by someone about an abuser, appreciating the time when she is not being abused. The comment reminded Nell of things said by wives of violent alcoholics: He's a nice guy when he's sober. Did Miss Mac write on the girls' records that they were good girls except when they were being bad? Nell doubted it, and made a note to locate the "Northern teachers" to obtain their testimony for the defense.

The girls' accounts of their questioning by Miss MacNaughton the night of the fire also struck Nell as odd. Except for Margaret Pridgen, only Edna Clark confessed to

100

actually starting the fires, and she had told Nell, "I told them I done it to get out of Samarcand." All the rest gave a response similar to Mary Bronson's. Pearl Stiles, the only one of the sixteen who resided in Bickett, insisted she knew nothing about the fire there, and "told Miz MacNaughton I did not do it, but she tried her best to get me to say I did."

Bertha Hall denied she confessed but did say, "If they took me back, there would be a fire."

Ollie Harding said, "I told her I knew about the first time (in Chamberlain), but I didn't help do it."

Estelle Wilson responded she knew Margaret Pridgen was going to set the second Chamberlain fire, but she had nothing to do with it and "I did not confess."

Chloe Stillwell said she did not confess, and "Miz MacNaughton never asked me anything about it." Three of the girls specifically claimed they were told by MacNaughton they were being sent to jail not for setting the fires, but for "other things."

Her interrogations completed, Nell had no doubt the girls had been truthful. Some of them, she suspected, especially Margaret Pridgen and Peg Abernethy, lacked the ability to deliberately deceive. Nell wondered why things had gone so terribly, terribly wrong at Samarcand under the supervision of Agnes MacNaughton. And she remained puzzled as to why so many of the girls had been accused of a crime they adamantly denied, while others almost proudly proclaimed their own guilt. Perhaps her scheduled interviews with Agnes MacNaughton and her staff would provide answers, but this was, for many reasons, a confrontation she wished she could avoid.

Early in May, May 4, to be exact, Nell again made the drive south to Samarcand. It was a beautiful spring day, not a cloud in the Carolina-blue sky. She could almost forget she had but two weeks remaining until the trial, with a great deal left to do. On this morning she ignored that uncomfortable reality and instead focused her thoughts on an attempt to reconcile her hopes for Samarcand with the girls' tales of beatings and mistreatment. Surely, she told herself, there must be some explanation. She had believed in Samarcand from its inception, believed it essential to fulfill her dreams for thousands of girls from among North Carolina's poor. She knew well how Samarcand operated, at least how it was designed to operate, for she had an insider's view. From 1922 to 1924 she had served as publicity director for the North Carolina State Board of Charities and Public Welfare, established by the legislature and given broad oversight responsibilities. Samarcand fell under the Board's jurisdiction, and Nell had written glowing accounts of its operation in the *News and Observer*, in news stories and her column. She had championed Agnes MacNaughton as the ideal superintendent, calling her "the right woman for the job." She knew the other members of the Board of Charities shared her hopes for Samarcand. Like Nell, they believed the school was helping improve the lives of girls who stayed there, transforming them into upstanding women. She knew they must be wondering what had prompted this group of girls to try to destroy the place and put Samarcand on the front pages of newspapers across North Carolina.

Although essential to her defense, Nell dreaded her appointment with Agnes MacNaughton. Under the circumstances, MacNaughton would inevitably view her as an adversary, perhaps both personally as well as professionally. Still, Nell hoped for an amicable and honest exchange, one which would produce a more definitive and nuanced view of the Samarcand fires and the reasons for them. MacNaughton was, after all, a career woman like herself, and should be fully aware Nell was diligent in her role as defense attorney, rather than embarking upon a personal vendetta.

Agnes MacNaughton approached her conference with Nell less with dread than with fear. It had been a horrible year, and with the trial approaching, things did not promise to improve. She felt her control of Samarcand threatened, slipping away from her. There had been considerable turnover on Samarcand's board of directors, most notably the loss of the Reverend A. A. McGeachy, board president, a position he had held from Samarcand's founding until his death last year. She was relieved that she would go into the trial with the continued presence of Leonard Tufts on the board in his familiar role as chairman of the building and grounds committee, She considered Leonard a neighbor. Over the years she had come to rely on his gifts to the institution, not just money, but also books, equipment, and cattle for the dairy herd. His Christmas season invitation to the girls to sell handicrafts, baked items and canned goods, to Pinehurst's guests, she saw as an example of his neighborly interest in Samarcand. Reverend McGeachy's staunch Presbyterianism, Leonard Tuft's recreation of a Scottish golfing resort at Pinehurst, and the region's cherished Scottish Highlands heritage, helped persuade her to come to Samarcand, a decision she had lately begun to question.

The girls, she felt certain, had told Nell Lewis a pack of lies about her and Samarcand staff members. Nothing she could do about that, but she had acted to rid herself of staff she deemed unreliable, firing three teachers only two weeks ago. In addition, just weeks before the arson, she had terminated three other unreliables, including the nurse. The rest of the staff, she believed, she could rely on. Her immediate staff, especially Estelle Scott, Claire Crenshaw, and Judy Ross, no doubt would support her unquestioningly.

Miss Mac watched as Nell's car pulled in front of administration building and Nell emerged. She stepped outside to greet Nell before she could reach the door.

"Miss Lewis, how nice to see you again," said Agnes, her voice crisp and lacking in warmth. "I hope you've had a pleasant trip."

"Yes, thank you, I did. And it is nice to see you again, Agnes, although I wish we could be meeting under more favorable circumstances."

"I assume you've spoken to the girls. I'm of course delighted you wish to speak directly with me. You can imagine what I've been going through."

"Yes, I have spoken to the girls at both Carthage and Lumberton." Nell detected a brittle edge creeping into Agnes' voice, and noted that her smile appeared forced.

"I'm certain you've been told some interesting tales. Girls, especially those girls, can have rather vivid imaginations," Agnes replied. "Let's go into the parlor where we can sit and carry on our conversation more comfortably." Passing through the reception area, MacNaughton re-introduced Nell to Miss Estelle

Stott, her personal assistant, a young woman whose facial features were framed by a shock of dark hair.

"A pleasure to see you again," Nell said, as she crossed her fingers when she told this lie to the woman the girls described as one of Samarcand's most enthusiastic disciplinarians. The parlor was a small sitting room next to the superintendent's office, furnished to make visitors feel at ease in the institution.

"Please take a seat." Agnes gestured toward an overstuffed floral Queen Anne wing chair. "Would you like coffee, or tea, perhaps?"

"No, thank you." Nell took her seat as directed while Agnes sat across from her on a small loveseat upholstered in matching fabric. "I hope you won't mind if I take notes as we talk."

"Not at all. As I said, I appreciate the opportunity to speak with you. And I appreciate your continuing support of Samarcand."

"I know yours is an extremely difficult job," Nell began. ""I can't imagine the responsibility it places on you."

"No, Nell, to be honest, you can't. But I am sure that you can imagine it is an extremely difficult and stressful position. As you know, the girls who reside here come from very troubled backgrounds. Even in the best of times working with them presents serious challenges, and these are hardly the best of times."

She paused briefly, but Nell waited for her to continue. "There simply is not enough money to run Samarcand properly. Funds for supplies, equipment, and staff were never easy to come by. But this Depression has created a crisis. Last year the legislature cut our budget dramatically. I can't replace broken equipment, so the beds and furniture in many of the dorms are broken, patched together to make do. We are short-staffed and many of those we hire leave as soon as they can locate a position with better pay, although I make every possible effort to retain them. I stretch our supplies budget every way I can think of, but it is difficult to replace clothing, blankets, dishware, and other such items that receive constant use. And adolescent girls have special hygienic needs, as you are aware, which are not without cost. Thank God we raise most of our food; otherwise the girls would probably starve."

Nell recognized Agnes' complaints as an opening defense, though much, perhaps all, of what she said was true. Her remarks were also, Nell understood, an attempt to steer the discussion away from any of Agnes' personal failings as superintendent. "I am, unfortunately, personally affected by the Depression and aware of its impact on others," said Nell. "I am sorry but not surprised to learn it has had such a terrible impact upon Samarcand. The fires, I'm certain, have only made the situation worse. Perhaps you could tell me a bit about them."

"Certainly. We were all eating supper, about six o'clock, when a resident in Tufts Hall, who missed supper because she was not feeling well, alerted Miss Moore, she's the matron of Bickett, that she had seen fire. Miss Moore proceeded to lead the girls from Bickett promptly, and in perfect order."

"Do you know how the fire in Bickett began?"

"It caught on the second floor, near the chimney, and could have come from a spark. But the staff became aware of a general rumor that the firing of Bickett was to be a signal to start more fires. Hilda Godley, a Bickett resident, told me Pearl Stiles

106

confessed to her that she had set the fire. I questioned Pearl, who denied it, of course."

"And the Chamberlain fires?"

"The first occurred about eight o'clock, probably set by a torch of fat pine and rags pushed through the ceiling, to the best of our knowledge. It was immediately discovered and put out, did no damage, though the girls were taken into the yard as a precaution. Miss Ross, the matron of Chamberlain, is a graduate of the Moody Bible Institute and is good to the girls." Ah, the Moody Bible Institute; Nell suppressed a smile as Agnes continued. "The girls were returned to Chamberlain, and some of them locked in their rooms. The second fire began much later, and appears to have been set in at least two places. We managed to get the girls out, almost fifty of them, but the building burned to the ground."

"You questioned the girls immediately after the fire?"

"We brought all the Chamberlain girls over to the Tufts Hall main reception area. We had to take them somewhere. The first thing I told them was, 'You must remember if you had nothing to do with this fire, stay out of this. But if you had anything to do with it, go into the teachers' reception room. All fifteen of the Chamberlain defendants went in."

"So you didn't question the girls individually?"

"Miss Stott, Miss Ross, and Miss Crenshaw were present when the girls were questioned. Several of the girls said, 'I did it.'"

"Were they told they were being questioned about a capital offense?"

107

For the first time, Agnes' voice reflected irritation. "I had no idea arson was a capital crime in North Carolina. I am not a lawyer, as you are. I don't dwell on such things. All I was thinking about was how to get the dangerous ones off the grounds, and save the rest."

"I completely understand." Nell tried to mollify Agnes. "May we talk a bit about discipline at Samarcand? When, for example, is corporal punishment used?"

"I expect you got some frightening tales from those girls," Agnes began. "But I can assure you, we try to use the least discipline necessary to retain control. Work is the main punishment, especially the more arduous tasks. Some of it is hard, dirty work, but it isn't dangerous and hard work never hurt anyone. I was brought up on hard work. Idleness is the devil's workshop, as they say, and that is certainly true here at Samarcand."

She adjusted the collar of her dress. "Our discipline depends on each individual case, and sometimes we have to resort to corporal punishment. But it is always a last resort, never administered in a manner to seriously injure the girl. So far as I remember, only two of the fire setters received corporal punishment." She leaned toward Nell. "Spare the rod and spoil the child. Foolishness is found in the heart of a child, that's what the Good Book says."

Nell resisted the temptation to argue Biblical interpretation with Agnes, for Bible study was a serious undertaking for Nell. "One other issue, and I'll be finished," Nell said, sensing she would continue to receive only defensive responses from Agnes, who was trying to stay one step ahead of her. "Can you tell me about personnel turnover, and if any staff have been released recently, especially just before or after the fires?"

"Staffing is always difficult. We try to obtain qualified employees, good Christian women, but these are hard jobs, emotionally draining, with long hours. As you know, the pay isn't much. So, yes, we experience significant personnel turnover. About ten days before the fire I was forced to release Arline James, Viola Sistare, and Lottie Mitchem. Soon after the fire it became necessary to release Charlotte Tedder, Fronie Harrell, and Marjorie Ferebee."

That's interesting, thought Nell. Six staff members given the door just prior to and immediately after the fires. A significant purging, when by her own acknowledgment, Agnes had great difficulty hiring. "That exhausts the questions I have," said Nell. "It has been a pleasure to see you again, and I want to thank you for your cooperation. Agnes, as I said, I can't imagine the difficulties you face in your position. And you know, of course, that I have always supported Samarcand's mission." Nell glanced about the room, seeking to end their conversation on a more cordial note. "This is an attractive room, lovely furnishings, I commend you on your taste. May I continue to use it to speak with a few of your staff?"

"Certainly." Agnes rose and extended her hand. "I know you wish to interview Miss Stott. I'll ask her to come in."

The studied severity of Estelle Stott's appearance surprised Nell, who found the woman's comical jerky gait amusing and a contradiction of her hairstyle. Her posture and facial expression exuded an air of aloof disdain which Nell chose to ignore. As expected, Stott added little to McNaughton's testimony, but what she said Nell found intriguing. In addition

109

to Pearl Stiles, Stott said, Hilda Godley claimed Lettie McGraw, Ruth Gray, and Elda Deweese had confessed to setting the fire in Bickett. It struck Nell as odd that none of the other three who supposedly confessed were sent to jail, but she decided not to press the issue.

Miss Stott also denied that Miss MacNaughton had spoken individually to any of the girls, but stated, "I warned the girls arson was a capital offense and they should be careful about what they said." She also said twelve of the girls "have all confessed to me to actually setting the buildings on fire." She added that three others, Mary Lee Bronson, Wilma Owens, and Pearl Stiles, "have confessed to knowing about the fires," but did not say they had confessed to her. When pressed on this issue, she admitted that Pearl Stiles had never confessed. For some reason Nell could not fathom, Miss Stott said that on the night of the fire, Pearl Stiles and another girl "would not sing to their house matron, but that night they laughed and giggled." Nell wondered whether Miss Stott considered laughter and giggles from teen-aged girls grounds for a charge of arson, and which songs the girls were supposed to sing for staff entertainment.

When asked about punishment, Miss Stott replied, "They don't average a whipping once a month, and we never whip a girl for just one offense." Whippings were administered judiciously, she insisted, and never harmed the girls. Like Miss MacNaughton, she claimed only two of the defendants had been beaten.

Miss Moore, matron of Bickett Hall, shed some light on why Pearl Stiles had been included among the defendants, although she was the only one from Bickett jailed and had consistently denied her involvement with the fires. Pearl, she stated, "had more demerits than anybody in Bickett Hall."

Nell last spoke with Judy Ross, matron of Chamberlain, the discipline hall. When the second fire began, according to Miss Ross, "About fifteen girls were locked in their rooms for running away." After their initial questioning, sometime close to midnight, the girls were taken to the jail in Carthage. Like MacNaughton, Stott, and Moore, Miss Ross insisted that punishment at Samarcand was mild and just. "We always try reasoning and persuasion. Corporal punishment is administered with a switch; we never use anything else now, although we did use leather." Nell stifled the urge to ask Miss Ross to describe the difference between a switch, a stick, and a tree branch.

Nell said her goodbyes quickly, again thanking the superintendent for her cooperation. She had no desire to prolong her visit to Samarcand, but felt instead an urge to leave it far behind. During most of the drive home, she tried to make sense of what she had heard. The testimony of the Samarcand staff even more firmly convinced her the girls were telling the truth. The staff had acknowledged they beat the girls with sticks and leather straps and locked them in their rooms as punishment. They agreed most of the defendants never confessed to being involved in setting the fires. They also acknowledged sending at least one of their most difficult residents to jail on hearsay evidence provided by another resident. There were conflicts in their stories. MacNaughton said she did not know arson was a capital crime, whereas Miss Stott said she had warned the girls of this fact when they were first questioned, with MacNaughton in the room. Miss Ross claimed she was not in the room when the girls were questioned initially, but MacNaughton said she was. MacNaughton said she never questioned the girls individually, but always in a group. Miss Moore claimed they were questioned individually, which supported the girls'

111

testimony. And it was clear that whether questioned in groups or individually, the girls had been placed under tremendous pressure to confess. The testimony of the Samarcand staff revealed serious issues, both moral and legal, enough, Nell thought, to begin to build a credible defense.

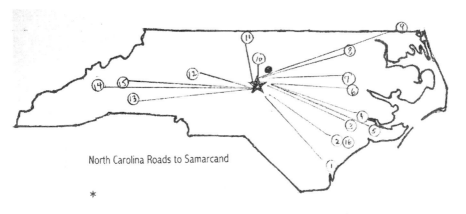

North Carolina Roads to Samarcand

North Carolina Roads to Samarcand

*
Samarcand   ● Raleigh

1   Wilmington-Pridgen
2   Kinston-Abernathy
3   Ayden-Mercer
4   Washington-Harding
5   Cove City-Seawell
6   Tarboro-Council
7   Rocky Mount-Bronson
8   Halifax-Clark
9   Norfolk-Hall
10 Haw River-French
11 Leaksville-Hayes
12 Lexington-Wilson
13 Rutherfordton-Mull
14 Waynesville-Owens
15 Canton-Stiles
16 Kinston-Stillwell

Nell Battle Lewis in Nice, France, with the YMCA in 1919,
when she enjoyed a romance with Lenoir Chambers.

Agnes B. MacNaughton, Supt.

1918 - 1934

Agnes B. MacNaughton,
Samarcand superintendent 1918-1934.

Miss Mac's terrier Jack with two Samarcand girls.

Bickett Hall, burned in 1931 arson fire along with Chamberlain Hall.

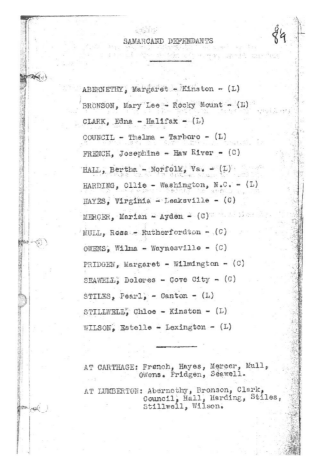

Lewis notes listing sixteen jailed Samarcand defendants.

DRAMATIS PERSONAE

The Ring:

    Miss McNaughton, Miss Stott, Miss Crenshaw.
    Possibly Miss Bradshaw and Miss Sourlock and Miss Ross.

Teachers Recently Dismissed:

    Before the Fire:
        Miss Viola Sistare, Miss Arline James and Miss Lottie Mitchem.

    After the Fire:
        Miss Charlotte Tedder
        Miss Fronie Harrell
        Miss Marjorie Ferebee.

Positions:

    Miss McNaughton, Superintendent
    Miss Stott, Miss McN's Secretary
    Miss Crenshaw, Discipline Officer.
    Miss Ross, matron of Chamberlain Hall.
    Miss Moore, matron of Bickett Hall.
    Miss Bradshaw, teacher in school
    Miss Sourlock, present school principal.

Lewis notes listing Samarcand staff.

ABERNETHY, Margaret

AGE: Was 17 on Dec. 8, 1930.

BIRTHPLACE: Durham

HOME: Kinston

PARENTS: Mother dead. Doesn't know mother's name
and does not remember her. Father took her
away from mother when she was about four
years old. Was told later that she was
dead. Step-mother, Willie Green raised
her. Was not kind to her, she says.
Father's name: Ivey Abernethy. Now
serving two year term in State Penitentiary at Raleigh for incest. Margaret the
victim. Father was a plumber.

BROTHERS AND SISTERS: No whole brothers and sisters
that she knows of. One half-brother died
in infancy. One half-sister five or six
years old. Another half-sister now a baby.

DISEASES: Usual diseases of childhood, measles,
mumps, whooping cough, etc. No serious
illness. No V.D., she says doctor said.

EDUCATION: Began school when she was six years
old. Attended irregularly. Stopped when
she was thirteen. Was in the fourth grade.

OCCUPATION: Never had a job.

DATE COMMITTED TO SAMARCAND: Dec. 8, 1928.

REASON FOR COMMITMENT: Mistreatment by her father.
Incest began when she was ten years old.
Continued at every opportunity when step-
mother was out. Father drank, but was not
drunk when he mistreated her, she says.
"It was against my will. He kept me scared".

ATTEMPTS TO ESCAPE: Twice

WHIPPINGS: Four. "They lay you down on a rug and
take straps or switches. If you run away
they cut your hair".

Lewis interview with defendant Margaret Abernethy revealing
father's incest and Samarcand abuse.

North Carolina's Central Prison in Raleigh at time of the Samarcand trial.

Margaret Pridgen (left) on Wilmington street with her mother and nephew after the Samarcand trial.

Margaret Pridgen
grave in Wilmington.

Nell Battle Lewis
grave in Oakwood Cemetery
in Raleigh.

Agnes Brown MacNaughton
grave at Bethesda Presbyterian Church in Aberdeen.

4

The Preparations

Why, Nell wondered, did everything have to be so difficult? As if she didn't have enough problems trying to cobble together a defense which had some chance of success, the defendants and her legal colleague seemed to be conspiring against her. Two days after her trip to Samarcand to interview Superintendent MacNaughton, front page headlines of newspapers across the state announced that the girls in the Carthage jail had staged a riot the last day of April, and in the process managed to set that facility ablaze. Where, Nell asked herself in exasperation, did these girls keep finding matches?

The headlines vilified her defendants as uncontrollable young savages on a rampage. Coming only two weeks before the trial, the sensationalizing presented Nell with a huge public relations problem. *News and Observer* reporter Carolyn Reynolds ran a more judicious blow-by-blow account of the jail fire, taken from her interview with the girls the day after the incident. Pleased to be the center of attention, the girls had spoken freely to Reynolds, describing their actions in detail, with Josephine French quoted as saying, "I'd like to get the thing in the paper just like it happened." Nell read Josephine's account with amazement and an increasing sense of frustration, not because she doubted Reynolds' reporting, but because of the damage she knew it was doing to her clients, who, of course,

121

were completely oblivious to the negative impressions created by such publicity:

> We were in the cell and asked the jailor's wife to let us out for awhile. They do let us out of our cells every day. There's a victrola upstairs and sometimes we dance. She said we couldn't. We wanted to get out and she said she'd see about it and went downstairs. She didn't come back so we set fire to one bunk—to bring somebody up to let us out. They came then—and let us out. We went downstairs. Some of us went one way and some another. They turned the hose on us; I don't know who they were. Sheriff McDonald nor Deputy Kelly were here. They were some of the firemen. Sheriff Kelly got here right soon and ordered the water turned off. We were as wet as drowned rats. The firemen said they weren't throwing water on us, they were putting out the fire. We went upstairs then and danced about two hours when we came back down here. The cells had been cleaned up and dry things put on the beds. Sheriff McDonald came in late. He brought us some dry clothes and everything that we needed. We sort of expected that we'd have to stay with everything wet and messed up. But we had dry beds and clothes and went to bed and to sleep.

After reading a lurid account in the *Moore County News*, Nell was grateful to Carolyn Reynolds for allowing Josephine French to speak. Under the headline "Samarcand Girls Riot in Moore County Jail," the local paper gave a far different account. The sensationalism continued in bold print above the body of the story:

Smash windows, Fire Bunks and Attack firemen, Five Girl Prisoners Created Much Trouble for Moore County Deputies, Do

Much Damage to Jail during Mutiny, Arm Themselves with Knives After Forced Released into Jail Corridors.

The narrative portrayed the girls as madwomen. Nell read in a state of disbelief, wondering if things could get any worse, "They found time to crash all the windows and tear out several of the heavy wire screens. Their faces mostly pretty, distorted with rage, their clothing disheveled, hair awry, and eyes gleaming, they seemed to be angered to the point of temporary insanity." Their antics, the story concluded, were witnessed by "practically the entire populace of Carthage" and set "the whole town agog." The appeal of the alarming story in the hometown paper far outweighed the more rational *News and Observer* report, and was carried by a number of papers across the state, which Nell found completely predictable.

The following day she learned that the public perception of the Samarcand girls indeed could get much worse, and had been dealt another blow by a totally-unexpected source. Among the accounts of the Carthage jail riot, one which ran in the *Wilmington Morning Star* was penned by, of all people, George McNeill, the court-appointed attorney with whom she would be sharing the defense for the Samarcand girls. It was similar to an account he had written Nell, and she could only assume he also had written to the parents of Margaret Pridgen, and they had given their letter to the local newspaper. However the paper obtained it, Nell faced the embarrassing fact that her co-counsel had described the Carthage defendants as "acting like raving maniacs, smashing windows and running around and perfectly nude. It was necessary to call out the fire department and throw water on them."

She wished she could disavow George's compellingly vivid description of the Carthage jail riot, but unfortunately, he had been on the scene. Still, she could not believe the man's naivete, how lacking in common sense the man was. She knew McNeill only by reputation as a competent but unimaginative lawyer who lacked the eloquence and showmanship required of a first-rate defense attorney. Upon finishing McNeill's account, Nell's astonishment quickly turned to anger. She was glad she was not possessed of a gun in a room with him, for quite probably she herself would soon be on trial for her life. There was nothing to do except to drive back to Carthage and try to explain to the girls how damaging their outburst was and that she would tolerate no more such misbehavior. She would also have to convey to McNeill the meaning of discretion, a concept which should be second nature to even the less astute members of the legal profession.

Nell met George McNeill in his office, small and unimposing, like the man himself. At least he's a stylish dresser, Nell thought, noting his neatly-pressed white shirt, patterned maroon and gold tie, and navy trousers with cuffs breaking slightly over cordovan wing-tipped Oxfords. "Miss Lewis, a pleasure to meet you, finally," he said in his best Southern gentleman voice, a thin smile on a thin face beneath thin black hair combed straight back with no part to reveal early balding.

"Nell, please call me Nell," she replied disarmingly. "We should be on a first-name basis by now."

"Of course, Nell. I assume you read my description of the girls' latest outburst in the Wilmington paper?"

Nell thought, at least he gets straight to the point. "Yes, George, I'm afraid so."

"I can assure you I never meant for it to be published. I only replied to Margaret Pridgen's grandmother. She has written me several times, seeking better treatment for Margaret. I wrote to assure her that Sheriff McDonald and his deputies, especially Deputy Kelly, agreed Margaret could easily be influenced by the other girls, and had placed her in a separate cell. I guess the only good news is that Margaret did not participate in the disturbance."

Good news for Margaret's grandmother, Nell thought, but it hardly mattered to anyone else. She started to say so, changed her mind, and continued the steel magnolia approach. "Yes, George, I've seen it, and to be quite honest, it presents a bit of a challenge, especially appearing so close to the opening of the trial." What an understatement, she thought, I may be the only defense attorney in the state to face the prospect of my co-counsel testifying for the prosecution. "But it's there, and there is nothing we can do about it now," she continued. "The question is how do we respond?"

"What do you have in mind?" George asked contritely, relieved that Nell seemed content to confront the situation rather than assign blame to him.

"Our only hope to avoid a conviction is to put Samarcand on trial and portray the girls as victims. Perhaps not totally-innocent victims, but victims nonetheless. Which they are."

"I completely agree, but that won't be easy."

"No, it won't be easy," Nell replied, "but it is possible. Samarcand is far from being a summer camp. Whatever it may have been a decade ago, there is plenty amiss today, and we can show that. Yes, I do believe we can portray the girls as victims, and rather effectively."

"I assume that means attacking Superintendent MacNaughton?" George had a slight rise in his voice.

"Especially by attacking Superintendent MacNaughton," Nell replied a bit more forcefully than she intended. "I have talked at length with each of the girls, and am convinced that what those girls endured gives us plenty of evidence with which to attack."

"She has many supporters, not just here but across the state," George replied. "You were one of them. Most of them will now stick by her, not wanting to see her feet of clay. That is just the way it works. You know this."

"I am all too well aware of this. Many supporters will be my friends and former colleagues from the State Board of Charities. I can assure you they'll not be happy with me, will regard me as a turncoat, and will have nothing good to say about either of us to anyone who will listen. That's why we have to turn this press coverage around, do damage control, get the girls portrayed in a positive light, not as young harridans.

"But how?"

"I'll speak to some of the *News and Observer* writers. The Reynolds story is more like what we need, something which treats the girls more sympathetically. If you have any press contacts you think might be helpful, speak with them. At least that's a start. We can't stand additional sensationalized stories. Above all else we have to make sure the girls stage no more such outbursts. That would kill us, or more accurately, quite possibly kill them."

126

"I'll see what I can do, try to find a local reporter who'll present the girls more favorably, victims of abuse, family neglect, that sort of thing. God knows they are."

"Good," said Nell, "that would help, but the admission of participating in the arson, made to reporters by several girls, does present a major problem. We can't afford any more of that. I think we should be prepared to offer a guilty plea for at least the three girls who have consistently admitted guilt, ask for a light sentence in return, and continue to make the case the others are not guilty. You think that's a sound strategy?"

"I've considered that a possibility, perhaps an inevitability," George replied. "A plea might work. I'm certain the State has no real interest in seeing sixteen girls, wards of the state, actually receive a death sentence. But the Attorney General's Office is serious about this case. I don't think we should tell them we are prepared to enter a plea for any of the girls at this point. And I doubt the Prosecution will accept a plea for some of the girls, but not for others. I am convinced they want the lot of them convicted and sentenced to serve some time."

"Fine," said Nell. "We prepare the best defense we can muster and bide our time on a possible plea. I've written Dr. Harry Crane, one of the state's most respected psychologists, a former member of the State Board of Charities and a long-time acquaintance. I've asked him to interview some of the girls, perhaps find evidence of diminished capacity, and he has agreed. I'm also writing to a number of former Samarcand staff, hoping to find testimony that corroborates the girls' claims of mistreatment. But for the moment, George, we need to make clear to the girls we can't have any more riots or jail fires. Their behavior is gaining them a statewide reputation. After the riot here, someone introduced a bill in the state legislature which I understand is going nowhere, thank God, to require that the girls be transferred to Central Prison."

"Well," said George, "let's go see them and read them the riot act." Nell smiled, but hoped his defense skills proved infinitely more polished than his sense of humor. Still, she remained pleased George seemed cooperative, and that they agreed upon a basic defense strategy. Together they set out to make certain the girls ceased their destructive behavior before the defendants made any credible defense impossible.

They met with five of the girls at Carthage. Margaret Pridgen continued to be held in a separate cell, her spirit broken by her transfer from Lumberton, and the realization she would not soon be going home. Virginia Hayes, still recovering from her "appendectomy," remained in her cell. The remaining five seemed delighted to see them, laughing, chattering, and welcoming them as if they had not a care in the world.

"Girls," Nell began, "we have come to talk with you about your trial. I think most of you have spoken with Mr. McNeill here, but for those who have not, he will be helping me conduct your defense. We wish to discuss the trial with you. But first we want to know more about the fire last week. Why in the world would you do such a thing?"

Josephine French spoke up immediately, as Nell suspected she would. She clearly saw herself as the group's spokesperson. "Miz Lewis, we just wanted to get out of our cell for a while. We were so bored we had to do something, make something happen. Starting a fire is about the best way. We started the fire to bring someone up here."

128

"You certainly succeeded," Nell said, amazed and exasperated by the naïve sincerity of Josephine's response. "You girls have to realize such actions are not helping us defend you. Just the opposite is true; you are making it very difficult. In fact, if something like this happens again, I'm afraid you will have to find someone else to take your case. I care what happens to you, but I want to win your case, not lose it."

"Please don't do that, Miss Lewis," begged Wilma Owens, another sixteen-year-old, but lacking in Josephine's aggressive attitude. "We really didn't mean no harm."

"Then why did the newspapers say you smashed out all the windows?"

"When the firemen came and turned on the water," Wilma explained, without a hint of deception in her voice, "a crowd began to collect and we decided to give them a show. But we didn't break half of what was broken. The men did it."

These girls don't comprehend what a dire situation they are facing, Nell thought. It's all fun and games to them: We didn't do it, the firemen did it. She could picture using that defense in court. "And what about the accounts that you found pocket knives and attacked the firemen with them?" Nell asked.

The girls responded with giggles. "Oh, that," said Josephine. "We just had two itty-bitty knives, found them lying on a table. Dull as butter spreaders, wouldn't neither one of them cut nothing. We didn't cut nobody. The man got cut hisself jumping out the window. We didn't try to fight nobody. We just wanted to get out of our cell for a while."

Great, Nell thought. Not only did the firemen break the windows, they cut themselves. She couldn't tell whether

129

Josephine was lying, whether her version of the incident was correct, or whether she believed it to be true regardless of what actually happened. It's hopeless, she thought, absolutely hopeless. She made a final attempt to get the girls to realize they simply must behave until the trial. "Girls, I am not joking. If there is one more incident of misbehavior, one more rampage, one more fire, I'll quit. Do you understand?

"Yes, Miss Lewis," came the unified response.

"Good. Then we will see you at the trial."

She and George left the room to shouts of "Goodbye, Miz Lewis," between spasms of girlish giggles. My God, Nell thought, where do they keep getting matches?

The following Monday morning, with exactly a week remaining before the trial, her exasperation with the girls replaced by a growing desperation, Nell met with Dr. Harry W. Crane, who had graciously complied with her request agreed to interview several of the Samarcand defendants, especially Margaret Pridgen and Margaret Abernethy. Nell had first met Harry years before as a fellow member of the State Charities Board. She liked and respected him, but most of all, she trusted him, which is why she had written to ask him to interview the girls. After experiencing the girls' immature judgment, Nell was fairly certain he would find at least some of the girls to be both emotionally and intellectually handicapped, enough so she might be able to build a case for diminished capacity. If she could use this argument to get the charges against even one or two of the girls dropped, that would be a small victory, so she hoped Harry had little good to report.

They met in her Raleigh office, and Nell was surprised by how Harry had aged since she last saw him. Never a robust man, he seemed much smaller, his now-grey hair complimenting his pale complexion. As she greeted him, she thought, perhaps his aging appearance reflects my own. Curious how we think of ourselves as always appearing the same age even as the years roll by. She remembered how startled she would be seeing her own face in the mirror, thinking, who is that woman? Can this be the same person who flitted around France, so in love with her handsome fiancé?

"Nell, I don't know how much my reports will be able to help your case," Harry was saying, bringing her back to the present. "There may be some material you can use, but on the whole, I don't think they are promising. I wish this weren't the case, because if ever anyone needed help, God knows these poor young girls do."

Impulsively, she reached out and took hold of both his hands, causing him to show a startled smile. "I can't tell you how much I appreciate your interviewing the girls, Harry," she said, letting go of this brief physical contact. "Why don't you just tell me what your findings are, and I'll be the judge of their legal merits?"

"Seems reasonable. You're the lawyer," he replied. "And before we begin, may I ask, how are you, Nell? I hope life is being good to you."

"I'm doing as well as can be expected under present circumstances," Nell replied. "It IS good to see you again. Why don't you begin with your report on Margaret Pridgen? She is the one I'm most concerned about, from both a legal and personal perspective."

"Oh, yes, that Margaret. She's the one who admitted to starting the Samarcand fires, correct?"

"Correct."

"She's a sad case, Nell. I spoke with her for some time. She seems withdrawn from the world, almost uncaring about her fate. I'd say she is severely depressed. This is situational depression, based on present reality. From what she told me, I think she really believed starting the fires would result in her being sent home.

"She had thought her family loved her, until they sent her away to this place which treated her so badly. She wonders whether the new baby girl in her household displaced her in the hearts of her parents two years ago. She was eager to go home to reclaim her rightful place, but now she realizes her rebellion against mistreatment has made it unlikely she will be sent home soon. She still doesn't understand how serious her situation is, that she may never see home again, or her little sister. Her family does care, and given Margaret's symptoms of depression, I can understand why they requested she be placed in a cell away from the other girls, and that she receive individualized attention."

Dr. Crane's description of Margaret's current state of mind caught Nell by surprise. "But Margaret Pridgen is the girl who claimed to be the leader of the Samarcand revolt, and proud of it," Nell said. "Margaret also led the rioting at the Lumberton jail, which got her transferred back to Carthage. If she's depressed, why did she act out this way?"

"Likely it has to do with birth order in her family," replied Harry. "Margaret is the oldest child, and the oldest child is born into the role of leadership. It may also have to do with her temperament. Some people withdraw when they are depressed; others become more extraverted. This is often the case with

132

people who display mania. They appear to be extraordinarily energized, but in reality they are fighting their depression with increased activity, trying to take control of their fate."

Nell found herself greatly affected by Harry's explanation, and wondered whether this dynamic might also apply to her own highs and lows. "I'm sorry to hear Margaret seems depressed," Nell said, attempting to hide her emotional response and realizing she should not allow herself to identify too closely with her client. "But I need to know your findings concerning her intellectual abilities."

Harry took a moment to observe Nell's demeanor, then answered, "I determined that Margaret is mentally retarded, to use a legal term, feebleminded. I conducted a thorough examination, including administering an intelligence test, on which she scored poorly."

This professional response surprised Nell not at all; rather, she had expected it, not because of her own experience with Margaret Pridgen, but because over the years she had witnessed the way those in positions of wealth and power describe the poor and unfortunate as mentally inferior, genetically incapable of managing their lives, not competent to make decisions which might impact the larger society. Her service on the Board of Charities taught her that labeling the poor, especially the rebellious poor, "feebleminded" provides a blanket excuse to control them for their own good. Professionals like Dr. Harry Crane unwittingly conspired to keep the poor in their place with diagnoses of feeblemindedness because this was the role for which society rewarded him.

Nell understood that the common cultural assumptions he brought with him likely influenced the results of his

133

examinations. In her biology studies at Smith College, she had come across the official scientific view that female brains are smaller than male brains, and therefore the natural order requires men to hold dominance over women. From her Biblical study she recalled Paul's admonition, "Let the women keep silent in the churches," quoted as justification for her own church's refusal to admit women to the pulpit. And North Carolina's public university at Chapel Hill denied females admission on the same basis as males. The same rationale justified white dominance over Negroes, that their brains were smaller than those of Caucasians. These determinations, of course, had been made by white men, who envisioned a male God the Father with a male Son the Saviour.

Margaret Pridgen might be the retarded girl Dr. Harry Crane described, but Nell had seen another Margaret, an adolescent of conviction and courage, as a last resort capable of organizing others to challenge institutional power they found brutal and oppressive. This was not the behavior of someone of slow mentality, and even a wild animal will attack when cornered, out of survival instinct. At Gastonia, Nell had seen striking laborers display courage and conviction as they sought more humane working conditions, only to be disparaged as lazy and crazy by those in authority. She had heard men who beat their wives justify the beatings by claiming, "She deserved it," just as those in charge of Samarcand justified physical assault on the arson defendants.

Even as she questioned the wisdom of Harry's diagnosis, it was, in fact, what she had hoped for, laying the basis for a key element of her defense. What mattered was not whether Margaret actually was feebleminded, but whether Dr. Harry Crane testified that she was. He was North Carolina's preeminent authority in the field, frequently employed by state institutions. If he testified Margaret was feebleminded, Nell could contend that Margaret was not guilty because of diminished mental capacity. And even if she were convicted, the court would take into consideration her mental state for purposes of sentencing. Dr. Crane should go a long way toward removing the threat of execution, and she was glad she had engaged his services.

"What about Margaret Abernethy?" Nell asked, hoping to receive a similar diagnosis.

"I'd say she has an IQ not much higher than that of the Pridgen girl. I determined her IQ to be 60. At the moment, she is more talkative than Pridgen, more alert, though she is hardly more aware of the circumstances she faces. But she definitely shows more spirit. After what she has lived through, that is a minor miracle."

"And the others?" Nell asked, anticipating additional support for a diminished capacity defense.

"Not much different, variations on a theme. I'd say they are all mentally slow, but there are some differences. Pearl Stiles has an IQ of barely over 60. Marian Mercer is a different story, and clearly the brightest of the four. There is a discrepancy in her records which made it difficult to determine her IQ. Marian gives her age at fourteen, while her mother says she is sixteen. If she is fourteen, her IQ would be 79, which would make her borderline normal. But if she is truly 16, then her IQ is 69, and she would be considered feebleminded."

"What is your opinion about her age?" Nell asked.

"In my opinion, the girl is at least sixteen, perhaps older. She is fully developed physically and speaks with the assurance of a somewhat older girl. But in any case, I would try to ascertain the correct ages for all four of the girls, as it is crucial to determining their IQs."

Harry continued, "There is one other thing. Both Margaret Abernethy and Marian Mercer told me they were examined by a psychologist at the Caswell Training Center before they were taken to Samarcand. It would be a good idea to contact the psychologist at Caswell and see whether you can obtain a copy of his reports. It would also be helpful, I think, if you find that these reports exist, to determine whether they were sent to Samarcand when the girls were transferred there."

"Thank you, Harry," Nell said. "That's an excellent suggestion and I'll follow up on it. I suspect there may be a good deal in the girls' records we are not privy to, and even more troubling, since much never entered their records which should have. It's a shame, really. We all had such high hopes for Samarcand, truly believed it could transform the lives of poor girls in difficult family situations. And God knows, with this economic Depression, their numbers continue to multiply."

"I still hold that hope for reform schools," Harry responded. "Which is why I've served on the Board of Charities for so long. But hopes and expectations are not the same. In my profession, I've learned all too well that Lord Acton was correct, absolute power does corrupt, and it can corrupt even the best intentioned among us. Prisons, reform schools, orphanages, it makes no difference. Institutions in which a staff has almost total control over a population offer the perfect opportunity for the abuse of power. That is what the professional literature teaches, and what my personal practice has proved to be true."

"A terribly bleak assessment of human nature, Harry."

"Nell, it's accurate. But it doesn't mean I've given up on the human race. We both know we must have such institutions to prevent chaos, and we will never make them perfect, but we can make them better. That's why I'm helping you, Nell. Certainly it isn't for the negligible expert witness fee I will be awarded by the court! You and I are of one mind; I hope my testimony can get the charges against the girls dismissed, or, if by some miscarriage of justice they are convicted, it will convince the court to spare them the death penalty and instead pronounce rather light sentences. Not to do so would be an outrage."

"I'm going to do my best to get them off completely," Nell replied. "I don't believe most of them belonged at Samarcand. Nor do I believe most were involved with setting the fires, and I do believe even those who did were under extreme provocation. Were I in their shoes, I probably would have set the place afire much sooner. The Samarcand they experienced was not the Samarcand we envisioned, and I intend to convince the court of this."

"Attacking Samarcand won't be popular with a lot of your friends," Harry said, surprised by the determination in Nell's voice.

"I've already spoken with George McNeill, the court-appointed attorney in the case, about this strategy, Harry. We won't be attacking Samarcand. We plan to focus on Agnes MacNaughton and her inner circle, to show they perverted the Samarcand you and I and others supported."

"As I said," Harry replied, "many of your friends won't like this, including those who served on the Board of Charities with you. Some continue to believe Agnes MacNaughton sits on the right hand of God."

"Evidently Agnes agrees with them."

"This isn't a joking matter," Harry cautioned. "Agnes MacNaughton has been at Samarcand since its inception, and she has made a lot of influential friends over the years. She knows on which side her bread is buttered, and she shows a different face to these patrons than she does to the Samarcand girls."

"I'm well aware of this. I've already heard from some of her friends, who are my friends as well, telling me I'm making a mistake taking this case."

"Fools rush in where angels fear to tread, Nell. And hell is likely to have no fury like Agnes MacNaughton scorned."

"Honestly, I don't have any other choice. It's not just a matter of finding a winning strategy. I have no doubt things have gone badly wrong at Samarcand, and Agnes is the reason. Far too much 'spare the rod and spoil the child,' mixed with more than a touch of sadism."

"From what I know of Agnes' life," Harry said, "I expect she's more than a bit repressed."

"She certainly hasn't been Queen of the May," said Nell.

"She'd be an ideal candidate for psychoanalytic treatment," replied Harry. "It would be interesting to know more about her life in Canada and Scotland, what motivated her to migrate to the United States. More significant, what prompted her to choose to work with young people labeled deviant. There are careers which are more appealing."

"Why, Harry," said Nell, "I might wonder the same thing about you! Why would you choose to spend your days making assessments of troubled people?"

"Touche'," replied Harry with a smile. "My own psyche could use some tuning up, no doubt, but it does not compel me to intentionally inflict pain on others. Quite the contrary, I try to alleviate their suffering."

"Some of these girls could be lying about their treatment, but not all of them," continued Nell. "With MacNaughton on the witness stand, I think I can prove what they endured at Samarcand provoked their rebellion, that it was actually self defense."

"I wish you luck." Harry gathered his notes and stood up. "I hope my reports help. I can't believe the court would seriously consider the death penalty for these girls under any circumstances. And if even part of what the girls say about Samarcand is true, I hope the court would never impose a prison sentence. Those girls have served time enough."

"I'd never contend the girls are helpless innocents," Nell said. "But I fully agree they have served time enough. Even if they are found not guilty, which I'll confess I think unlikely, few of them face a pleasant future, and God knows, most have endured a hellish past."

Harry looked up at Nell with a final comment. "Whatever the outcome of the trial, Nell, I hope your defense will provoke a public outcry for an investigation of Samarcand and similar institutions. I believe we must have them, unfortunately, but I also believe we have a duty to see they are administered as humanely as possible."

Agnes McNaughton and her administration certainly failed to meet that criterion, Nell thought, as she watched Harry walk into the hall. She had an impulse to go after him and invite him for lunch at the nearby Mecca Restaurant, but realized they would be observed by some of Raleigh's movers and shakers, and she did not wish it to be said they were in collusion of a personal nature.

With his reports now in hand, Nell had but one remaining major task on her list of things she must do before the trial, and that was to interview several former Samarcand employees, especially those terminated recently. Tracking them down had been difficult; some had been impossible to find. She had obtained the addresses of eight and written to them all; five had replied to her letters. Two replies were useless, only brief statements that the respondents had worked at Samarcand and been dismissed sometime in the spring of 1931. The other three were more promising, two especially so. Though brief, they contained detailed and damning comments about the manner in which Agnes MacNaughton ran Samarcand. It took some pleading, but Nell had convinced the three to meet with her in Raleigh to provide detailed, witnessed, accounts of their experiences

On the day of this group meeting Nell was anxious, worried her witnesses might not keep their appointments. With the trial only days away, she would have no time to reschedule, and she needed their testimony. They were the only adults who could, or would, corroborate the girls' testimony about their treatment at Samarcand. MacNaughton and her "ring," as Nell referred to Miss Stott and Miss Crenshaw, would certainly tell a far different story.

Nell arrived at her office early, made herself a cup of coffee, and reviewed the written responses. At just after ten, she was relieved to hear a knock on her door, and she quickly ushered the three women into her office. Lottie Mitchem, one of the teachers the girls felt treated them well, was a small, birdlike woman, while Fronnie Harrell was tall and lean, her sharp features framed by bobbed salt and pepper hair. Imposing in stature, with an almost military bearing, Bessie Bishop had served as the Samarcand nurse during 1929 and 1930. Nell decided to first speak with Miss Mitchem. "Miss Lewis, for years I've read and enjoyed your column in the *News and Observer*," said Miss Mitchem. "It was with great satisfaction I learned you are to defend these girls charged with burning the two buildings at Samarcand."

"How nice of you to say." For a moment Nell considered the possibility that all three women might be regular readers of her column. She quickly realized it more likely they all were simply being polite.

She started to ask Miss Mitchem her general impression of Samarcand, but before she could phrase the question, Marjorie

Ferebee gushed, "I taught high school there for almost a year, you know, lived in a cottage with the girls. I enjoyed my work, found it quite pleasant. I found them to be like girls everywhere, except perhaps a little less polished. When they arrived, they were cheerful and carefree, and had a lot of what you call 'school spirit.'"

Upon hearing this, Nell had a sinking feeling. "You found the girls enjoyed Samarcand, Miss Ferebee?"

"Oh, no, Miss Lewis, I don't mean to give that impression. It's that I want you to know the girls at Samarcand were very little different from girls I have encountered in other situations. They are just girls, no more, no less, as you and I were girls. After awhile they became dissatisfied. They longed to go home. It seemed to me they couldn't understand why some girls could come and stay only a few months, while others were never allowed to leave."

"That's something I'm not clear about myself," said Nell.

"As I understand it," Miss Mitchem said, "Samarcand was established mainly for the purpose of helping underprivileged girls, supplying the training which their homes failed to give them. In all honesty, I must say that in some respects I think this purpose is being fulfilled. But there is something about Samarcand, an atmosphere, a feeling, which undermines all the correct principles so vital in the training of children."

"I'm not sure what you mean by that, Miss Mitchem. Could you please be a bit more specific?"

"Why, certainly. In the first place, the girls are looked upon by some of the teachers as prisoners sent as punishment for crimes they have committed. Often this is thrown up to the girls

142

if they seem the least bit resentful. Another thing, the girls are driven rather than led to do what is right. This is effective for some, of course. Some are naturally more difficult than others and require a sterner approach. But for a larger number this approach only creates a sense of rebellion."

"I agree with you completely," said Nell, "and the fires certainly prove your point."

"There were other problems directly related to the manner in which Samarcand was administered," Miss Mitchem continued. "Minor deeds, which almost any girl might do, are stressed, while matters I consider of much greater importance are ignored. Also, there are no definite rules, which leaves both staff and the girls in a state of confusion. Each teacher has her own code, and it seems hard to expect the girls to remember all of them."

"The girls are punished for breaking the rules?"

"Oh, yes. Rather frequently."

"Did you witness them being punished?"

"To be honest, no, I never saw them being punished, if you're referring to corporal punishment. Miss MacNaughton, Miss Stott and Miss Crenshaw did all of that. Still, if all I have heard is true, the punishment is entirely too severe. I heard, mostly from the girls, they are forced to lie upon the floor on their faces while they are viciously beaten with thick switches. I do know sometimes they are locked in a small room with only a blanket to sleep on the floor."

"What you have heard, Miss Mitchem, conforms exactly to what the girls have told me. I doubt you find that surprising," said Nell.

"Unfortunately, I don't, Miss Lewis. I want you to know that in speaking with you today, I am only thinking of the girls. I expect they may need a great deal of help, and wish you the best of luck."

"I appreciate your taking the time to do so, and you have been a great help. If you would like you may remain in the office waiting area, or, if you prefer, take a stroll about town while I question the others. There is a little Greek restaurant around the corner." Miss Mitchem chose to wait.

Nell spoke next with Fronnie Harrell, a nice woman who also announced her admiration for Nell's newspaper column, but added little to Lottie Mitchem's impressions of Samarcand. She confirmed that conditions were poor, girls beaten, and Agnes MacNaughton's actions often erratic and high-handed. Nell quickly focused her questions on MacNaughton's dismissal of Harrell soon after the fires. "Do you know why you were dismissed, Miss Harrell?"

"I have no idea, and frankly, I was surprised, as were the other two teachers dismissed the same day, April the 14. We all told Miss MacNaughton we hated to leave her without teachers so near the end of term. She said not to worry; she was going to stop school anyway. She said she needed the girls to work in the fields, and besides they were too far behind in their work to graduate or pass their grade. We asked if our teaching had been satisfactory, and she said yes, and she didn't blame any of us for the girls being behind and would give us recommendations."

Nell sensed Miss Harrell would be unlikely to provide additional relevant information, and asked if there was anything she would like to add to her statement. "Not really," Fronnie replied. "Except Miss Stott carried us in the truck to Southern Pines to meet the bus. Miss MacNaughton told us goodbye as we were leaving Samarcand and shook hands with us. Nothing else to say, really."

"Thank you, Miss Harrell." Nell said. "I want you to know how much I appreciate your coming to speak with me. You have been a great help, I assure you. If you wish, you may sit with Miss Mitchem while I question Miss Bishop."

Nell was relieved that Miss Bishop did not tell her how much she also enjoyed her column in the *News and Observer*. Nell began the interview by asking how long Bessie Bishop had worked at Samarcand. "I came as the school nurse in August 1929, and I left in July 1930, after the school term expired," Bessie answered.

"You were there for a full year?" Nell asked, recalling that Margaret Pridgen had arrived at the school in June 1929.

"Yes, and I would have been delighted to have gone back, had conditions been such that I might have done what was good for the girls."

"You didn't feel conditions at Samarcand allowed you to do this?"

"No, I didn't." Bessie's matter-of-fact tone shifted to reveal disapproval bordering on disgust. "When I went to Samarcand conditions were terrible. I was never allowed to act on my own judgment and had I carried out commands I was given continuously, it would have proved disastrous for the girls under my care. My reports were criticized and I was instructed to write them in a manner certain to please the governing board. There

145

were hardly any panes in the windows, girls had to sleep in their wards in the cold. Most beds were broken and were propped on chairs, blocks of wood or anything available. I was ordered to place the blocks so that visiting board members might not see them."

"Are you saying there was a deliberate effort to keep board members from knowing the truth about how Samarcand was operating?"

"I am saying it was deliberate, and it was constant."

"But times are hard, Miss Bishop," Nell said, playing devil's advocate. "Perhaps new window panes and furniture are difficult to come by."

"I'm sure that is the case, but that is no reason to deliberately deceive," Bessie continued. "And it wasn't just supplies and equipment that were a problem. Sanitation was very poor. At times girls were forced to lie on the floor. Just one example: there was an epidemic of scabies in the school, and no accommodations for the girls at all. They were sent to the hospital daily, five and six at the time, no beds for them.

"I was told to put them on the floor. I objected; the weather was cold, no sheets, no pillows, very few blankets. Superintendent MacNaughton informed me this was good enough." Not surprising, Nell thought, as Bessie paused for a moment. Agnes MacNaughton grew up in Scotland before moving to Canada. She probably didn't think North Carolina had a real winter. Besides, Nell ruminated, I've slept on a pallet many times, and been perfectly warm and comfortable. "She said it was better than what the girls were used to at home," Bessie continued. "She didn't seem concerned about the girls' health. I asked her whether we could isolate the scabies patients

146

in one hall until we got the outbreak under control. She said that would not be considered under any circumstance, so the infected girls went back to their dorms. As you can understand, we never got the epidemic under control." Nell could hear anger in Bessie's voice and did not interrupt her. "For the entire eleven months I was at Samarcand, I was refused tooth paste or brushes. Once I ordered them myself and the hospital and I gave them to the children. I was admonished and was told the girls had no need of such things.

"Venereal disease is the menace of all such institutions. In Samarcand it was rampant, and no wonder. The girls having gonorrhea and syphilis were thrown together, using the same dishes, lavatories, bath tubs, and bath cloths. Their clothes were not isolated and neither were they. I asked if the infected girls could be put in a separate cottage, and Miss MacNaughton informed me that was the most absurd thing she had ever heard, it was perfectly fine for them to be together, and one could not get it from another in any way. Inevitably, girls who came having tested negative for venereal disease became positive for gonorrhea and syphilis, and many of them taken off treatment would have to be put back on."

Nell found this almost unbelievable, but continued to take notes. "And the dog bites. I was not allowed to report treatment of dog bites. Miss MacNaughton said the board would not approve of it."

"Dog bites?" Nell was incredulous.

"Yes, dog bites. I treated numerous dog bites caused by Miss MacNaughton's dogs. She had two, a collie named Laddie and a terrier named Jack. Nothing could be said or done about the dogs. Miss MacNaughton even would send Laddie to the hospital for treatment as though he were one of the girls, but I refused to do it, and so Miss MacNaughton would come and administer the treatment herself. She used up on the dogs our precious supplies meant for the girls. And burns, the girls came in for treatment of lots of burns, all obtained while cooking. If she were there, the superintendent would order me to refuse treatment. If she were not there, I treated them."

Nell had expected testimony about corporal punishment, but what Bessie Bishop was telling her was almost beyond belief. According to Bessie, Agnes MacNaughton was a tyrant, with no regard at all for those in her charge. "Do you think Superintendent MacNaughton was deliberately cruel to the girls?" Nell asked.

"At times, yes. But she was also ignorant of medical considerations, sometimes shockingly so. In such incidents she had no hesitation in substituting her judgment for mine. For example, this girl who had epileptic attacks suffered a seizure and I had her carried to the hospital. Miss MacNaughton came over and laid into me for having her carried to the hospital, threatened beatings for her, and doing other things, too. The child was unconscious and cyanotic, and remained unconscious for the rest of the day. The Superintendent threatened to pop her jaws if the child did not speak to her, but the girl could not speak at all."

"Do you think Superintendent MacNaughton is ignorant of epilepsy?" Nell sought a rational explanation for Agnes' behavior.

"Miss MacNaughton was ignorant of a great many things," Bessie replied. "Either that, or completely uncaring about the girls' health, which, I am sorry to say, some of her behavior

148

clearly indicated. Once Dr. C W. Durham, who called at Samarcand, instructed me to isolate a girl with diphtheria. I did, placing her in the isolation room which was so small you would almost suffocate in it, but all that we had. Miss MacNaughton came to the hospital and wanted to know where the girl was. I told her I had placed her in the isolation room on the doctor's orders. 'I don't care for doctor's orders,' MacNaughton said, 'and I will not stand for that at all.' She took the child out and sent her to the playground to join the other girls. MacNaughton would punish girls by locking them in a room with this child, who was a menace to others and feebleminded as well."

Nell caught her breath. "And did you witness other types of punishment, physical punishment?" she asked.

"Oh, yes, many times. Once a girl showed me great black and blue bruises on her body and I asked 'How in the world did this happen, did you fall?' and she said, 'Have you not heard? Miss MacNaughton beat me almost to death.' On many occasions girls came for treatment for bruises obtained from beatings by the authorities. Once I was told to carry a child to Chamberlain, the discipline hall, and to make sure she was 'warmed up.' The child was forced to lie on the bare floor, on her face, hands over her head, while MacNaughton and her staff held her down and beat her unmercifully with a leather strap. They termed it getting a spanking, but it was a beating. I hate to say it," Bessie continued, "but Superintendent MacNaughton thought more of her dogs, and treated them better, than she did the girls.

"Surely, you can't mean that."

"I'm afraid I do," Bessie replied, "for I saw it was the case. The terrier, Jack, was held up as not just a mascot but as an example for the children. On occasion the girls were carried to the chapel for Sunday School, only to be bawled out and told how low-down they were, what vile circumstances they came from, what evil they had done outside. Then MacNaughton would read dog stories to the girls and have one of her staff hold up the dog. She would ask the girls if they did not wish they were as good as Jack. There were parties given for this dog, who was entertained in ways the poor girls never were. The girls hungered for human love and attention, but it was the dogs who received it."

As Bessie finished speaking, for a moment Nell sat in stunned silence. She had expected the nurse to corroborate stories of the girls receiving severe beatings at the hands of MacNaughton and others, but never had imagined such an outpouring of tales of unspeakable behavior.

Bessie sensed her shock. "I assure you, Miss Lewis, that all I have said is true. And I could give you many more examples of what I believed to be appalling conditions at Samarcand and totally unacceptable behavior by the Superintendent and some of her staff, especially Miss Stott and Miss Crenshaw. That is why I left at the end of my contract. I will be happy to supply you with the names of other former staff who can verify that what I have said is true."

"I don't mean to imply that I doubt you, Miss Bishop," Nell said. "I'll take the names, but don't expect I'll be able to reach any of them before the trial. Your coming forward is an enormous help. I can't tell you how much I appreciate it."

Nell saw the three women off and slumped behind her desk. It had been quite a morning. She tried to make sense of their statements, especially those of Bessie Bishop, having no doubt the woman was telling the truth. What reason did she have to lie? If she were lying, she would hardly be so

150

forthcoming with the names of former staff members she believed could support her testimony. Yet Nell found it difficult to reconcile Bishop's testimony with the perception she once held of Agnes MacNaughton. She knew her as a severe woman, but not a cruel one. She understood professionals had differing opinions about corporal punishment, but clearly its use at Samarcand had gotten out of hand. Agnes MacNaughton faced a difficult challenge to keep the institution running in the face of financial cuts resulting from the Depression, this was indisputable. Lack of funds, however, did not explain her behavior toward the girls, her denigration of them, her disregard for their educational progress, and most importantly, her seemingly complete lack of concern about the state of their health.

Something had gone dreadfully wrong at Samarcand. Either Agnes MacNaughton was never the woman Nell and other members of the State Board of Charities had believed her to be, or she had she drastically deteriorated. To the girls of Samarcand, it didn't matter which might be true, and Nell wondered how many girls over the years had been abused with Miss MacNaughton at the helm. She also wondered whether Agnes was passing on abuse she herself had once suffered. Perhaps this was why she had left Canada to live in the United States, to escape bad memories. Or perhaps she had a dark side, a lack of empathy for other people. This type of person often was drawn into positions of authority over those viewed as unworthy.

Claire Crenshaw had once worked as a circus animal trainer. She sensed a linkage of Claire's background, her long-term association with Agnes, and Bessie Bishop's stories about Jack the Terrier having an unsavory connotation Nell did not wish to explore. She decided to stop plumbing the psychological depths of Agnes MacNaughton. Leaning back in her chair, she glanced up at the clock on the wall. It was 1:30, well past time for lunch. She considered going to the Mecca, but thought better of it. She had plenty of work to do, and besides, the events of the morning had left her with no appetite.

Nell penned a letter to George McNeill confirming their basic courtroom strategy. They had all the elements of a good case for the defense. She added that they could argue the girls should never have been incarcerated at Samarcand. Few had committed a crime; the vast majority were guilty only of behaving with boys in a manner of which some of the family disapproved. Others stood accused of potentially behaving in such a manner. She could show the girls endured horrendous treatment at Samarcand, and the girls had no legal way to prevent, or even challenge, this, as they had no credibility with the authorities, their mail was censored, and any visits from family members were supervised and strictly limited. Nell could use expert testimony that some of the girls suffered from diminished mental capacity. She could argue that only three of the girls, whose mental capacity was described as the most diminished, had actually admitted to setting the fires at Samarcand. She could prove the girls were treated both physically and legally in a manner the state had forbidden incarcerated adults to be treated. She could, in sum, contend that while some of the girls might be guilty of setting the fires, Agnes MacNaughton's administration of Samarcand, as an agent of the State of North Carolina, was the proximate cause of their behavior. It was, she knew, an unorthodox strategy, but it was the only one open to her. And besides, Nell was convinced, as she picked up her pen to write George, it was sad but true.

5

The Trial: Prosecution

Nell sat alone in her hotel room. She had driven down from Raleigh to Carthage late Sunday afternoon, hoping to review her case once more, enjoy a good night's sleep, and rise on Monday morning May 19 relaxed and prepared for trial. But things had not gone as planned; she hardly slept, was up by six, and found herself peering out her window at a charming view of Moore County Courthouse across the street.

The courthouse square itself was historic, not the building Nell saw before her. The square was the heart of the town, its reason for being. This had been so since 1814, when the residents of Moore County placed a crude log courthouse on the site. Constructed at a previous location three decades earlier, before the town of Carthage had been laid out, the log courthouse was the first of five to occupy the square. Four previous structures had been destroyed by fire, which Nell found ironic, considering the arson trial which was imminent. This present courthouse, a rectangular, three-story edifice built ten years earlier of Indiana limestone in a modified Renaissance design, was deceptive, for it appeared to have existed for more than a century. Massive stone steps led to each of four entrances which faced the four major streets converging on the square. Manicured swaths of spring green grass bordered the building framed by large old oaks, lending a gracious, less governmental appearance. The panorama would have made a perfect Norman Rockwell cover for *Saturday Evening Post.*

She found courthouse squares quaint and bucolic, especially in small towns like Carthage, appropriate for a place which served as a repository for the records of the daily life of the county's citizens—births, marriages, deaths, transfers of property by sale or bequest, payment of taxes, all the mundane, routine events which imbue life in such communities with a feel of changelessness. In reality, life in counties like Moore was always in a state of flux, and courthouse activity reflected these significant changes. The recent stock market crash which had shattered the usual tranquility had led to a flurry of foreclosure proceedings and delinquent tax payment notices, and was but another of the crises endured during the more than a century the five courthouse incarnations had served the citizens of Moore County.

As a newspaper woman Nell was well aware that the courthouse record-keeping function, even in the best of times, painted a distorted picture of community life. What occurred inside the courtrooms portrayed life in the county on a broad canvas, as a more tumultuous, violent story, filled with the passion and fury of human relationship. The buildings which stood on Moore County Courthouse Square had witnessed a constant parade of human strife—murder and rape, shootings and stabbings, arson, burglary and theft. These events, too, were woven into the fabric of community life. The courthouse, some might be tempted to say, by now had seen it all. Nell knew better. Moore County had never seen anything like the trial of the Samarcand girls, which would begin in little more than two hours.

The Rainbow Restaurant, a gathering place for courthouse employees, local attorneys, habitués, and downtown shop owners, opened early. Nell slipped into a booth at just past

154

seven as breakfast clientele were beginning to gather. She didn't bother to read the menu, as menus here were redundant. She ordered two eggs over easy, with grits, toast, and coffee. Her order arrived just as George slid into the booth opposite her. "Breakfast?" Nell asked.

"No thanks, I've eaten."

"Coffee then?"

"Why not? I'll probably need it." George placed an order for black coffee.

"Hope you don't mind if I eat while we talk. I'm starving."

"Not at all. Go right ahead."

"You think we're ready?"

George paused a moment. Nell could sense him thinking. "I really believe we are. Nothing else we can do."

"We have a bit of a problem," said Nell. "Bessie Bishop can't make it to the trial, but the testimony of Lottie Mitchell and Fronnie Harrell should be more than adequate. The girls, will they be ready?"

"I hope so. I've done everything you asked. Ladies from Presbyterian and Methodist churches are helping to dress them this morning, probably at the jail now. I've seen the clothes your friends sent, practically new and all stylish, but not over the top. Ladies will see that the girls look their best. They'll look better than they ever have in their poor, miserable lives. Some, I suspect, will clean up good and be quite attractive."

"Not too attractive," said Nell. "Don't want them to appear seductive and wayward. Let's hope they don't find any matches on the way here."

"Gallows humor?"

"Lord, I hope not." Nell was surprised by the bite in her tone. She shifted quickly to her professional voice. "Given any more thought to waiving the right to a jury trial?"

They had discussed this possibility earlier, after learning the trial would be before Superior Court Judge Michael J. Schenck. Nell had never met him, but she knew he was considered to be North Carolina's preeminent trial judge. She had researched his background because a smart trial lawyer is wise to scout the territory. Like many of the state's prominent citizens, Schenck's family had connections to the textile industry, although his father, himself a judge, had left law to become a railroad executive in the post-Civil War era. Younger Schenck's biography was typical of a male from a leading North Carolina family. In 1897 he had graduated from the University of North Carolina in Chapel Hill, the alma mater of her fiancé Lenoir Chambers, where her own family's name, Battle, was writ large in history. UNC was the favored institution of higher education for the sons of the state's elite, although the daughters were not admitted for study. Schenck traveled to Cuba soon after the Spanish American War to take a position with the American Insular Civil Service, which he held for two years. Returning home, he again enrolled at the University of North Carolina, this time in law school, graduating in 1903.

After graduation, Michael Schenck, a single man at age 27, opened his law practice in Hendersonville in western North Carolina, eventually becoming mayor. In 1909 he met and married a woman named Rosa Few and started a family, which would eventually include two sons and a daughter. In 1913, Governor Daniel Craig appointed him to a five-year term as Solicitor for the 18th District, prosecuting criminal cases in several mountain counties. During World War I when Nell was abroad with the YMCA enjoying romance with Lenoir, Schenck was serving stateside as a major in the Judge Advocate General Corps, and with the war's end in 1918 he resumed his law practice. In 1924, Governor Cameron Morrison named him Superior Court Judge. Two years later he won election to an eight-year judicial term.

Nell first learned of Judge Schenck during her service on the State Board of Charities, when she discovered his writings about a justice system for wayward youths. Instead of placement in a reform school, Judge Schenck argued that upon arrest juvenile offenders should be able to post bond and report weekly to a "man of exemplary precepts." While some criticized his idea as a return to the apprentice system, Nell saw considerable merit in his proposal, especially in its efforts to involve the state's most respected citizens with the youth of the state who most needed their advice and attention. His reputation as a reformer gave her some hope, but she knew him by reputation only and had no insight into the kind of person he was. She would have to rely on George's measure of the man. "George," she said, "what do you think of Michael Schenck? The man inside the robe, not the man holding the gavel. You've known him for more than twenty years. Is he the type of person upon whom we should place our bet?" George stared into his coffee cup, as if an answer to her question resided somewhere near the bottom.

"Wel-l-l," he drawled, still searching for the appropriate response, "he's rather complicated. I know you must be familiar with his ideas about how to reform the juvenile justice system, but don't let that mislead you. He's a very serious person, some would say stern. Let's just say he's not a man who would whistle in elevators."

157

"And in the courtroom?" Nell asked.

"What you would expect. Always in command, brooks no nonsense. Likes to ask questions from the bench. Tremendously respected by other judges, and assigned the hard cases throughout the state, has been for years. I suspect our case is the reason the Chief Justice sent him here for this superior court session. Knows the law and follows it, doesn't legislate from the bench, but is fair and understands the difference between justice and the letter of the law. I'd say that about sums him up."

"What's your final decision on waiving jury trial?"

George hesitated a split second. "I'd say do it. God knows, you can never guess what a jury will do and the local press has been pretty rough on the girls. We've an experienced judge and a fair one, someone we know has expressed sympathy for troubled youth and questions the effectiveness of reformatories like Samarcand. I don't think we can expect to do better than this."

Nell picked up the check. "Let's walk over to the courthouse and see whether we can get the prosecution to agree to a waiver."

"Don't think that should be a problem," George said. "Prosecutors known how fickle juries can be, and they probably expect some pretty damning testimony about conditions at Samarcand."

As she was paying the fifty-cents which included George's coffee, Nell glimpsed a school bus pulling up in front of the courthouse. She handed the cashier a dollar. "Keep the change," she said. "Let's go, George, it's show time."

Other customers mobbed the cash register, trying to pay their checks and rush to the courthouse. Before Nell and George

158

could cross the street, a sizable crowd, mostly reporters and photographers, had emerged from restaurants, stores, and parked cars, and was descending on the bus. Nell spotted Bess Thompson and a photographer from the News and Observer pushing toward the front of the crowd. She and George moved up the courthouse lawn so they could see over the heads of the reporters who now surrounded the bus. As they waited for the bus door to open, the crowd continued to grow, swelled by the idle curious who had come to town for the excitement of the trial, perhaps to catch a glimpse of the notorious Samarcand girls. The door opened, and a deputy sheriff stepped down, imploring people to make way, pushing them back until he cleared a semicircular space at the foot of the bus steps. He motioned to the girls to follow him, and led them out one at a time. Before the first girl's feet hit the ground, the crowd surged forward and flashbulbs popped. Some spectators yelled out at the girls, who began to yell back. Nell winced when she heard a few unladylike curses from her clients, and she was glad they mostly kept their composure. Again the deputy pushed the crowd back, this time with his night stick in hand, clearing a path.

Mary Lee Bronson was the first off the bus. The sight of her took Nell's breath away. She wore a black rayon spring shift which flattered her youthful figure. Her hair, blonde and cut slightly longer than a page-boy, curled softly at the ends. "My God," Nell murmured to George, "she looks like a young Greta Garbo." Edna Clark followed Mary Lee, stepping smartly. A pretty brunette, the seventeen-year-old wore a navy blue dress with a bias-cut skirt, a light blue scarf slung casually over her shoulders.

"I told you your friends had sent some stylish clothes." George said. "Playing dress-up with these girls, I suppose. You

159

women!" The other girls filed out of the bus, following the deputy through the crowd, smiling, laughing, exchanging an occasional greeting with onlookers, shouting to newspaper photographers. Rather than seeming sheep to slaughter, the bevy of defendants might well have been off to a dance at St. Mary's School. Even poor little Margaret Abernethy, wan and thin, was presentable in a yellow cotton floral print. Nell felt apprehensive that the girls showed no contrition for what they had done. Cockiness would not serve them well before Judge Schenck.

"Well, George," she said, "we're off and running."

The Courtroom

The grandeur of the Superior Courtroom caught Nell by surprise. She took it all in, for she had not expected to find this in a provincial courthouse. Much larger than the chamber of the North Carolina Supreme Court Courtroom in Raleigh, it boasted a thirty-foot ceiling from which hung several large gilded brass chandeliers. The judge's dais, jury box, and witness box were made of polished walnut. On the judge's dais the flag of North Carolina flew from a pole to the left, the American flag on the right. In front of the dais sat the clerk's table and chair, made of the same highly-polished wood. To the right of the Judge's dais was the jury box within a polished wooden rail separating court functionaries from spectators. The prosecutor's table was on the left of a swinging gate separating spectators from counsel tables, defense on right. The witness chair was to the left of the judge's bench. Opposite the jury box was an identical area for seating the grand jury, which was used at trials for witnesses, police officers, and sheriff's deputies. Facing the judge's dais were several rows of wooden benches which resembled church pews. The crowd of reporters, photographers, and curiosity-seekers, some no doubt hoping to be chosen as jurors and earn a day's pay, filled the benches and spilled out into the aisles.

Nell and George walked down the center aisle between the spectators' benches, aware of heads turning to watch their progress. Nell felt butterflies begin to flutter in her stomach, perspiration on her palms, and wondered if George had the same courtroom jitters. Was it because this was her initial case, or did the nervousness come with every case argued, every time, before a judge or jury? She prayed her nerves would calm as the trial began. She and George placed their brief cases on the defense counsel table at the same time.

The prosecution team had already arrived. "This is F. Donald Phillips, Solicitor of the 13th District," said George. "Solicitor Phillips, Miss Nell Battle Lewis."

"A pleasure to finally meet you, Miss Lewis, though I feel I've come to know you through years of reading your column."

"Thank you, Solicitor Phillips," replied Nell. "And my pleasure to meet you."

"This is Walter Siler, representing the State Attorney General's office," said George.

"Walter and I are old friends, George," Nell interrupted. "In fact, I read law under Walter in preparation for my bar exam. Well, Walter, I must say I never expected to be in a courtroom with you so soon, and certainly not on opposite sides in such a significant case."

Walter smiled warmly. "Nor did I, Nell, but you never know where the law might take you. This should be an...

161

interesting... experience. It is always good to see you. And to see you again, George. Sorry I can't wish you luck on your first case, Nell."

"You could agree to honor our request for a waiver of a jury trial," Nell responded. "I'm sure you and the solicitor have as much confidence in Judge Schenck's abilities as we do."

Walter shot a quick look at Don Phillips, who nodded yes. "Our pleasure, Nell, if you're sure that's what you want. The State, after all, has every interest in seeing justice done here."

"Thank you, Walter," said Nell. "I'm sure justice is what we're all seeking."

An excited buzz rose from the spectators, cutting short the pleasantries between attorneys. Nell turned to see the girls being escorted into the room, still smiling and waving occasionally to the crowd, and glancing about in hopes of finding a familiar face. She was thankful they were more demure than outside the courthouse, and amazed by the transformation the church women had performed. Styled hair and a hint of color on jail-sallowed lips and cheeks did wonders. The sheriff's deputy ushered the girls into the jury box, motioned for them to be seated, and with the matron sat behind the girls as the crowd's excited chatter died down. Deputy Sheriff Kelly, designated bailiff, entered, followed by Sheriff McDonald, three deputies, and witnesses scheduled for both prosecution and defense. In the grand jury box with the witnesses was a lone member of the local press, a reporter from the *Sandhills Pilot*. Nell wondered what privileged relationship accorded this reporter special treatment not bestowed upon his colleagues.

Promptly at 9:30 the doors to the presiding judge's chamber opened. Judge Schenck strode into the courtroom, accompanied by the bailiff. He took his seat in the highbacked chair behind the bench. His receding hairline and spectacles underscored his fifty–five years, and his robe covered what appeared to be a tall, still-fit frame. He rapped his gavel and directed, "Mr. Bailiff, open Court."

Deputy Kelly intoned in a nasal voice, "All rise. The Honorable Superior Court for Moore County is now open for the dispatch of business, the Honorable Judge Michael J. Schenck present and presiding. God save the State and this honorable Court. Be seated please and remain silent."

Judge Schenck again rapped his gavel and addressed all assembled. "I am aware this trial has generated considerable attention. Given the seriousness of the charges and the unprecedented nature of the defendants, that is perhaps to be expected. Before we proceed, I wish to make clear rules of conduct in the courtroom and outside in the halls. I see many members of the press, some with cameras, as well as a number of citizens of the community." He began holding up the fingers of his left hand one by one, as he ticked off the rules. "This is an open trial and everyone is welcome, but you cannot take pictures in this courtroom or otherwise disrupt the proceedings. Do not attempt to talk to witnesses until they have been released as witnesses. Do not attempt to talk to any of the defendants until this trial is over. Do not disrupt the court by outbursts or loud talking. Members of the families of any defendants may talk with them after court is recessed for the day, by arrangements with the bailiff and matron." George McNeill rose and stood quietly until recognized by Judge Schenck. "Yes, Mr. McNeill?"

"Your Honor, I wish to introduce to the Court Miss Nell Battle Lewis, who is with defense counsel and making her first appearance as counsel in a court."

Nell rose, nodded, and said, "Judge Schenck, it is my pleasure to appear in your Court."

"Miss Lewis, welcome to this Court, and welcome to the Bar," Judge Schenck replied. "Although we have corresponded only a few times, your name is well known to me through your column, which I have read more than incidentally."

Nell was amused by the play on words and glad to discover Judge Schenck had a sense of humor. She wanted to reply, "I'm glad you're one of my fans," but she simply said, "Thank you, Your Honor."

"Mr. Wilcox, will you read the Bill of Indictment to the defendants, and the court will take an entry of their pleas?" said the judge.

The Clerk stood, opened a file, and read the grand jury's bill of indictment, rendered only the day before. "The Jurors for the State, on their oath do present," plodding through the names of the sixteen defendants, proceeding to the first count of the capital offense of arson and the second count of attempted arson.

The clerk's presentation completed, Judge Schenck asked, "At this time, are the defendants ready to enter a plea?"

"We are, Your Honor," replied Nell. "To the Bill of Indictment and all counts, the defendants, and each of them, enter a plea of Not Guilty."

"A plea of not guilty having been entered, and trial by jury having been waived, is the State ready to proceed?"

Don Phillips rose. "We are, Your Honor."

"Call your first witness."

"The State calls Miss Estelle Stott. Please come forward, Miss Stott."

Nell turned to George and whispered, "That's a surprise. I thought they'd lead with MacNaughton."

"Probably saving her for what they expect to be a more dramatic moment," George replied.

Nell watched Estelle Stott walk rigidly to the witness stand. Her plain ankle-length black dress made her appear even more severe than when she and Nell had met a month earlier, but less haughty. Seated and sworn in, she began her responses to the Solicitor's questions.

"Miss Stott, please state your name and address and occupation for the record."

"I am Estelle Stott. I reside in a private apartment on the Samarcand Manor campus at Eagle Springs, North Carolina. I am the personal assistant to the Superintendent of Samarcand Manor, Agnes MacNaughton."

"Briefly, please tell the Court the purpose of Samarcand Manor."

"It is an institution owned and operated by the State of North Carolina, located in Moore County. Its purpose is to take into its confines and premises young women and girls who are living troubled lives and may be sexually delinquent. It is our mission to rehabilitate them to a wholesome moral life, teach them useful domestic skills, and inculcate in them the principles of the Holy Bible."

"How long have you served as assistant to the Superintendent?"

Miss Stott drew herself erect. "I am proud to say for three years."

"Prior to assuming this post, what was your training for this position?"

"Before coming to Samarcand, I worked at several correctional institutions in the northeast, the last being Sleighton Farms in Pennsylvania, under the direction of Martha P. Falconer. Sleighton Farms is considered a model institution, and Miss Falconer is widely recognized as a national leader in promoting enlightened reform institutions for young women." Miss Stott briefly smiled. "It was she who recommended Miss MacNaughton for the superintendent's position at Samarcand."

"Were you on the premises of Samarcand on the evening of Thursday, March 12, 1931?"

"I certainly was. "

Nell leaned forward. "Please tell the Court what, if anything, occurred around 6:30 P.M.?"

"I was in the dining hall with Miss MacNaughton and other staff members, having just finished dinner. It was approximately 6:30 P.M. The young women had eaten dinner. One of them, in the Tufts Cottage, apparently spotted a fire in Bickett Residential Hall near the chimney and roof, and came racing into the dining hall to alert us. Miss MacNaughton requested I go to Bickett to help insure the girls were safely evacuated and under control. By the time I arrived, the fire was spreading rapidly."

Miss Stott looked at the defendants. "My main concern was the safety of the girls in Bickett Hall. Miss Crenshaw rounded up the girls and got them out." She took a breath. "We attempted to put out the fire, but it was too late. Smoke filled the campus, and we were fearful the Bickett fire might set other fires. All we had for fire fighting was an old pump truck which would not operate. We have requested adequate fire-fighting equipment, but have not received any. By the time we called Carthage Fire department, the Bickett fire had largely consumed the building."

"Did you or any of the staff believe the fire at Bickett had been set by any of the girls?"

"We began to suspect this, but we had nothing to go on at that time. We were engaged in moving the Bickett residents to a safe place. Around 8 P.M. a fire broke out at Chamberlain, another residential hall. This time, we knew it must be arson."

George McNeill rose to object. "Your Honor, the witness had no way of knowing the fire was arson."

"Objection sustained. The motion to strike is granted. The witness will refrain from stating a conclusion. The Court will ignore this remark."

"Please continue, Miss Stott," Solicitor Phillips said patiently.

"That fire was small and extinguished within minutes by our farm workers using buckets. Then, toward 9 P.M., the second fire broke out. Miss MacNaughton called Sheriff McDonald, and he and Deputy Mudd arrived in about 30 minutes. By the time they arrived, the fire in Chamberlain was roaring." She paused for effect. "It could not be stopped. The fire

167

truck from Carthage still had not arrived. Both buildings, you understand, are wooden frame structures of cedar, two stories high, covered with wood shingles, and divided into residential rooms. We had a stiff March breeze that evening, so they burned rapidly."

"Did you have any suspects or girls rounded up at that time?"

"Yes, our troublemakers were all residing in Chamberlain Hall." She again looked at the defendants. "They were the girls being disciplined for breaking our rules. We immediately suspected them and took them to the Administration Building. I warned all the girls to keep silent if they had nothing to do with it. I took notes, with Miss MacNaughton and Miss Crenshaw present."

"Miss Crenshaw is an employee at Samarcand?

"Yes. Miss Crenshaw is the discipline officer at Samarcand."

"Please continue."

Miss Stott complied. "Several of the girls came forth and made statements. Margaret Pridgen was the first to confess. Then the others said they did it. Margaret Abernethy confessed. Others said they knew about it. Margaret Pridgen said Marian Mercer helped start the fire. I recorded their statements. When Sheriff McDonald and Deputy Mudd came, we brought the girls into the Board Room and they were questioned at length. You have these notes which I turned over."

It was obvious to Nell that Miss Stott had been well practiced in her testimony. "Now, Miss Stott," Solicitor Phillips said, moving closer to his witness, "this is a crucial point. Were both the residence halls at Samarcand, those which burned on the night of March 12, occupied at the time?"

"Yes, sir, both were occupied," Miss Stott said firmly. "As a matter of fact, some of the girls in Chamberlain were abed when the second fire broke out."

Phillips stepped back from the witness, turned and pointed at the defendants. "Is it your testimony here today, that two occupied dwellings were set afire by one or more of these defendants on the evening of March 12?"

"That is my testimony, Mr. Phillips."

"Is it your testimony further that other defendants assisted in the setting of the fires?"

"Yes, sir, it is."

"Anything you wish to add, Miss Stott?

"Well, yes. I want to say that all these girls have been treated well with kindness at Samarcand. My personal aim and that of the entire staff is to protect and improve them so they can return to society as useful Christian citizens. When these fires started, we all had the duty to protect those girls and young women who had nothing to do with the fires. We had to find out who endangered everyone and separate them from the rest."

Nell glanced at the defendants, who rolled their eyes at the words "kindness" and "protect."

"The State has no further questions for this witness, Your Honor."

"The defense may cross-examine," said Judge Schenck.

169

Nell felt her stomach do a quick somersault. She swallowed hard to relieve the dryness in her mouth which was accompanied by the familiar sweet taste. She sipped from the water glass on the defense table before she stood to question the woman with whom she had been acquainted for almost a decade and for whom she once held respect. As an unmarried professional woman, Nell knew the loneliness which Estelle Stott must often experience, having no spouse with whom to share the burdens of her days. She also understood the financial constraints facing Samarcand, and the difficulties of working with an underpaid staff and almost three hundred pre-adolescent and adolescent girls, all of whom came from seriously troubled homes. But these considerations did not justify the cruel treatment which was the proximate cause of the fire-setting. Quite the contrary. The State had a duty to provide a welcoming, merciful environment to compensate for the neglect and abuse in the families from whence the girls came. Nell could not recall any spankings, beatings, or other corporal punishment ever taking place in her own Christian home, yet somehow she and her brothers had managed to grow up well behaved.

"Miss Stott," she began, "I regret that we meet again under these circumstances."

"As do I, Miss Lewis."

"Now for the record, Miss Stott, will you tell the Court how long, and in what capacity, we have been acquainted?"

"We first met just after I came to Samarcand, when you visited with some members of the State Board of Charities, and again last month when you came to interview staff members."

170

"Thank you. Please tell the Court how many girls you had under your charge as of March of this year, and the range of their ages?"

"In March we had 276 girls at Samarcand," answered Miss Stott. "Their ages ranged, as best I know, from 9 to 21 years. We cannot legally keep women over 21 years of age. By then, their habits are formed, and we can do nothing more to protect them from themselves."

"Are the girls grouped so the young girls are not living with the older ones?"

"It is not always possible, Miss Lewis. We have limitations on our budgets, especially under current economic conditions. But we try. Each girl has her own bed."

"Miss Stott, are you familiar with the statutes under which inmates, prisoners, are committed to Samarcand?"

"Yes, I'm familiar with the Code of North Carolina and the provisions relating to Samarcand, though I wouldn't say I have mastered every detail."

Nell's took on a sharper tone. "Is it correct to say that a girl must first be convicted of specific enumerated crimes before she can be sentenced or committed to Samarcand?"

"The statute requires a conviction and commitment based on a conviction."

"Isn't it a fact, Miss Stott, that under the North Carolina Criminal Code, no girl or young woman can be sent to Samarcand without first being convicted of one of the following crimes: fornication, adultery, keeping a house of ill-fame, or a bawdy house, or violating the state laws as to chastity or vagrancy?"

"Yes, Miss Lewis, that is a fact."

"And do you know the offenses for which each of these sixteen girls on trial here today was convicted and committed to Samarcand?"

Don Phillips was up quickly. "Objection, your honor."

"Where are you going with this, Miss Lewis?" asked Judge Schenck.

"If it please the Court, Miss Stott says she is familiar with the law. She is the primary assistant of the Superintendent at Samarcand and has custody of these girls. I want to ascertain whether they were in lawful confinement at the time of the commission of the crimes with which they are now charged." Estelle Stott's iron maiden demeanor appeared to weaken as she listened to Nell.

"Objection overruled. But Miss Lewis, you must show relevancy. The witness will answer the question."

"I cannot be expected to recall the reason for the conviction of all these girls." Stott's voice wavered before she recovered her composure. "It is our practice at Samarcand, and has been from the beginning, that when a girl is admitted, she sheds her old life and begins a new life. To this end, when a girl is committed, the only statement on her record relating to any crime is one word, Delinquency."

Miss Stott had just confirmed what Margaret Pridgen had told Nell about being forbidden to acknowledge her own life experience. It was a convenient way to keep secret any abuse suffered by the girls, in order to protect those who might have violated them. If they were raped, they could not mention their rapist. If their father or grandfather or brother came into their bed and forced them, they could not acknowledge the violation of their bodies. They could not speak of their pain. Nell felt her sense of outrage resurface. She said indignantly, "You cannot tell me what the offense or offenses of which Margaret Pridgen or Wilma Owens or Edna Clark or Chloe Stillwell was convicted prior to her commitment to Samarcand?"

"That is correct."

"Do your records anywhere show the crime each girl is convicted of at the time of commitment?"

Miss Stott said archly, "We do not get a copy of the court proceedings, only the commitment and where it comes from. We ask our residents to forget the past so we can help them begin a new life. They are, in a sense, reborn from a state of sin into a state of grace." She added, "We are all born in original sin, and that was the purpose of Christ's crucifixion, you realize, to die for our sins and be resurrected into Heaven. We try to emulate the Christian way."

Nell cringed when she heard Miss Stott's references to religion, for in her column Nell took issue with the Christian concept of martyrdom and original sin, especially when victims are blamed for the sins of their perpetrators. But she knew better than to quarrel with Miss Stott's views, as this trial was taking place deep in the Bible Belt where such attitudes prevailed. She said evenly, "Are the commitment papers disposed of when an inmate comes to Samarcand?"

"My understanding is that the court records about the charge are not retained."

"What about the nine-and-ten-year-old girls taken in? Surely your records show reasons for committing those so young? Surely these children have not committed crimes?"

"Miss Lewis, sometimes there are cases when a parent or next of kin arranges with local authorities for unruly girls to be placed here before their undesirable habits become well established. As you know, we are charged with reforming these girls, and are not responsible in the least for their commitment."

Judge Schenck spoke before Nell could respond. "Miss Lewis, are you now saying that because some of these girls may not have been properly committed, they are now immune from prosecution? If that is the case, I remind you this trial is not a habeas corpus proceeding."

"Judge, I have interviewed all these girls, and am convinced many of them were never sentenced by due process of law. Furthermore, during confinement many have been cruelly treated and their times of commitment have been arbitrarily extended."

Solicitor Phillips was on his feet before Nell finished speaking. "I object, Your Honor, and move to strike that remark as being prejudicial, with no proof offered."

"Granted." Judge Schenck looked directly at Nell. "Miss Lewis, if you can show me law which says a mistake in a commitment is a defense to crimes committed by the person while in custody, I'd be glad to see it. This would be a novel theory, I'll grant you, but find me some law. Otherwise, I'm ordering you to refrain from this line of questioning."

"Yes, Your Honor. I have questions about humane treatment of these defendants by those holding them in custody."

Again Phillips leapt to his feet. "Objection by the State."

"Mr. Phillips," responded Judge Schenck, "this is cross-examination. Proceed carefully, and with a bit less legal creativity, Miss Lewis."

"Thank you, Your Honor. Miss Stott, is corporal punishment used at Samarcand, and specifically, has it been used on any of these defendants?"

"Yes, corporal punishment is used, but sparingly where there are serious and multiple violations of our rules." Stott's voice again tightened. "Escaping or attempting to escape would be examples. It stands to reason we cannot reform girls who remove themselves from our care."

"For the record, how many escapes normally occur in a year's time?"

"We average approximately two escapes a month, mostly in the spring and winter. The Superintendent has statutory power to issue state-wide arrest for any escapee, and they are usually caught within hours by Sheriff McDonald and his deputies."

.   "I see." Nell paused before asking, "When you say 'corporal punishment,' what exactly do you mean? Please describe this practice in detail for the court."

Nell caught a flicker of anger in Stott's facial expression before she responded in a controlled tone. "When an inmate has violated our rules after a warning, and does it again, the report comes to Miss MacNaughton and she orders a whipping to be carried out with a staff member administering the whipping and the number of blows. The inmate is laid out face down on a rug, to protect her from the floor, and is punished with whips cut

175

from a tree, usually with ten to fifteen licks. We do not spare the rod."

Nell thought but did not say that they used a rug not to protect the girl from the cold, hard floor, but to protect the inanimate floor from the blood of the living girl. She again cringed when she heard the Biblical reference. A murmur ran through the spectators as some defendants winced from the memory of their own beatings. Nell saw Judge Schenck shift in his chair. Reporters scribbled notes. The bailiff looked down at his shoes.

"Have you ever personally administered any beatings?" asked Nell.

Phillips again was on his feet. "Objection to the word 'beatings', Your Honor."

"Sustained. Miss Lewis, refrain from characterizing the corporal punishments. Let the witness answer."

"To rephrase," Nell continued, "did you personally administer the, to use your own term, whippings, or to use Judge Schenck's somewhat less descriptive term for the same action, corporal punishments?" As she spoke, she realized she should not show sarcasm because it might prejudice the judge, but she could only manage just so much restraint in the face of the whitewashing taking place courtesy of Miss Stott. For a moment, she thought how much better for her to write a column about the abuse at Samarcand, than have to compromise the truth in a courtroom.

"Yes, I have administered whippings, as have other staff members and, of course, Superintendent MacNaughton, who, I believe, originally administered all corporal punishment," said

Miss Stott, carefully parsing her words. "But as I stated earlier, whippings are rarely used, and always restrained both in force and in the repetition of blows." She glanced around the room. "Corporal punishment has been successfully used in many reform institutions across the country. At Samarcand it is rare."

A chorus of hisses and groans and murmurs of "Liar!" erupted from the defendants, to which the crowd responded audibly and sympathetically. Judge Scheck brought down his gavel, quickly restoring order. "Young ladies," he said, speaking directly to the defendants, "such outbursts will not be tolerated. Deputy, please see that the defendants heed this warning."

Nell thought, it's a good thing the girls do not now have matches, for they'd be tempted to set this courtroom afire in the face of Miss Stott's dishonest characterization of the abuse they suffered at her hands. She resumed, "Then it is your testimony that the corporal punishment administered at Samarcand is similar to the manner in which a child might be disciplined by a parent at home?"

"Yes, exactly," Miss Stott replied with a slight smile. "While they are at Samarcand, it is our duty to act as their parents. And I take that responsibility seriously, as do the Superintendent and all the staff."

"You stated a moment ago that originally Miss MacNaughton administered all corporal punishment at Samarcand, is that correct?"

"That is correct."

"I take it this practice has changed?"

"Samarcand was assigned increasing numbers of girls, so the Superintendent was forced to change that policy, for she

177

could not possibly mete out all the discipline she found necessary."

Nell made a mental note that Miss Stott had implied Miss MacNaughton's increasing use of beatings, which raised a doubt as to whether the beatings actually were effective as a prevention measure. "During the last few years, was corporal punishment ever administered by more than one person?"

"Yes, but only if the girl resisted violently."

"Sometimes by two persons?"

"Yes."

"Sometimes by three persons?"

Stott's voice dropped. "Yes."

"Sometimes by four persons?"

"Only in the most extreme cases," Stott said almost in a whisper.

"I'm sorry, Miss Stott, but I couldn't hear your response. Would you repeat it, please?"

"I said yes, but only in extreme cases."

A gasp shot through the spectators as the mental image formed of something akin to an adult gang attack upon one helpless young person. Again the judge banged his gavel and called for order.

"Only with the most violent and aggressive inmates," Stott hastened to explain, clearly affected by the response of the audience. "I'm afraid you have no concept of how strong and physical some of the girls are, Miss Lewis, or how violent they can be."

178

"And when three or more persons were employed at this task, isn't it a fact that one administered the 'whipping' while the others held the child down?"

Again gasps, then low mutterings, from the spectators, and again the judge banged his gavel. "There will be order in the court."

"Yes!" Stott answered defiantly.

"Like parental discipline at home?"

"Objection, Your Honor," Phillips said immediately.

"Sustained. Miss Lewis, I realize this is your first trial, and these are rather unusual courtroom circumstances. But I can assure you this judge can follow points developed through the examination of a witness, without counsel having to interject unwarranted asides. Do I make myself clear?"

"Yes, Your Honor." replied Nell, and continued to question Stott. "Tell us, is it customary to pull the girls' dresses above their legs when the whippings are administered?" She heard an intake of breath from the spectators.

"Objection, Your Honor," came immediately from Don Phillips. "I fail to see how the positioning of the girls' dresses is relevant."

"The witness has testified that whippings were moderate," said Nell. "The amount of clothing they wore would directly relate to the effect of each whipping."

"Objection overruled, but I caution you, Miss Lewis, tread carefully with this line of questioning. The witness will answer the question."

"Yes. Their dresses were pulled up when whippings were administered."

"And they were struck on the thighs and buttocks?" Again a murmur swept the courtroom, and reporters took notes.

"Primarily on the thighs, but only occasionally, and sometimes unintentionally, on the buttocks."

"Your Honor, I must object to this line of questioning," said an obviously concerned solicitor.

"I agree, Mr. Phillips. Miss Lewis, please move to another line of questioning, if you have one."

"I do. Miss Stott, were any whippings ever so severe as to require the punished person to be administered medical care?"

"If an inmate complained, a teacher sent her for examination, but only as a precaution."

"Have you or members of the staff required other girls to witness or participate in the whipping administered to a girl?"

"We do at times require the girls to witness whippings, thinking it serves as a good lesson for those who might be tempted to violate rules," said Miss Stott. "At one time we infrequently required residents to administer punishment, but we stopped that practice years ago."

"Miss Stott, isn't it a fact that corporal punishment has been abandoned and prohibited at most reform institutions, including the institution where you were formerly employed in Pennsylvania?"

"I understand that to be the trend."

"And isn't it also a fact that corporal punishment has been prohibited in state prisons, including those of North Carolina?"

"Perhaps." Stott's face flushed with anger. "But Samarcand is not a prison. As I have explained, corporal punishment at Samarcand is administered cautiously, the same as it would be in a loving home." Stott looked out at the spectators. "When I was a child, I myself occasionally was corrected with a smart slap or a switch on my legs. This discipline had no lasting bad effects, but to the contrary, taught me to keep to the straight and narrow." Some spectators chuckled, while another round of groans, but no shouts, arose from the defendants, and one girl suppressed a giggle.

"One further question on corporal punishment: Look upon the defendants and tell the court how many of them you know were punished by whippings?"

The girls leaned forward. Stott faced straight into the crowd, avoiding eye contact with the girls. "Miss Lewis, you know we don't keep records of corporal punishment. I do know that both the Abernethy girl and the Pridgen girl, and I believe I recall the Bronson girl, were punished for misbehavior. One or two others, perhaps, Josephine French, maybe."

"Was confinement in a locked room also a sanctioned punishment?"

Stott responded quickly, as if anxious to move on from the subject of whippings. "Sometimes it is necessary to isolate and confine inmates to give them a chance to reflect upon their conduct and attitude. This meditation is commonly regarded as effective."

"Is isolation often used at Samarcand?"

181

"More often for habitual offenders and only for those in our punishment cottage." She looked quizzically at Nell. "We cannot allow our residents to run wild and create chaos. We must keep order and respect for authority. What would you have us do?"

Nell ignored the baited question. "Are some of the girls confined in locked rooms for long periods, such as for one or two months?"

"Sometimes it is necessary to impose confinement to reinforce a lesson. The release from confinement depends on conduct of the person."

"Would that be 'yes' as to periods of confinement up to two months?"

"That's possible, Miss Lewis, but you have to remember that some of these inmates are not always truthful in their reports."

"Observing the defendants here today, do you know whether any were under lock and key when the fires broke out "

"I'm certain a few were locked up on that day."

"Were you aware that at least one of those girls was released by another girl prying the locked door open with a spoon?"

"No, I have not heard that, but it is certainly possible. There was a great deal of confusion, as you can imagine, Miss Lewis."

"Now on to a different subject." Nell pressed her fingers together. "Would restricted diets be used as a part of punishment for any girl in confinement?"

"Yes, but our restricted diets are under supervision of our nurses and medical staff. It is never just bread and water."

"Do you ever order the cutting of a girl's hair as punishment?"

"In very rare cases has this been done. I can only recall one or two cases in recent years."

"Do you know whether this was done to one of these defendants?"

Miss Stott adjusted the front of her collar. "Miss Lewis, I don't know what these inmates told you, but it is possible."

"How about different clothing being assigned to girls in the 'punishment cottage'. Is this a Samarcand policy?"

"Yes, we do impose a different dress code for inmates being punished. They have to earn their way out by good behavior."

"And would you explain to the court what a 'punishment cottage' is, Miss Stott?"

"It is one of our cottages set aside for those who repeatedly violate the rules."

"And which cottage is designated as the 'punishment cottage'?"

"Chamberlain Hall."

"Is Chamberlain one of the buildings which burned on the evening of March 12 of this year?"

"Yes. And Bickett Hall."

"Allow me to ask you, Miss Stott, how many girls were assigned to the punishment cottage on March 12?"

Miss Stott paused before answering. "About forty."

Nell counted on her fingers. "That would be, let me see, one out of every six or seven girls in residence. That's rather a high rate of misbehavior in a well-run institution. Of the sixteen defendants, how many were residents of the punishment cottage?"

Before answering, Stott paused to look at the defendants. "Fifteen were residents of Chamberlain Hall. Pearl Stiles, I believe, was a resident of Bickett."

"Miss Stott, you have testified that when an inmate was assigned to Samarcand, your records on that inmate did not indicate what crime she was committed for. Is this correct?"

"That is correct. Our policy is to close the door on the past, and look forward. The word 'delinquency' is put beside her name."

"Well, do you recall that I came to your administrative offices and examined the records of these girls just a few weeks ago?"

"Yes, I recall that we opened our files to you."

"Were you aware that on the files of several of these defendants, someone had made an entry beside the girl's name which said 'Bad' or 'Very Bad'?"

"No, I did not know that. But these girls are inmates and, frankly, some have bad behavior. Extremely bad behavior, sometimes violent, behavior. These girls are not in Samarcand without reason, Miss Lewis, as you very well know. They are not little angels."

184

Nell ignored Stott's hostile tone and personal reference. "Do you think when new staff members, or members of the Board, or an outside person sees the words 'Very Bad', they might be prejudiced against that girl?"

"Miss Lewis, you have never tried to operate a reform school, have you?"

Angered by Stott's obviously increasing hostility, Nell responded, "I ask the questions here, Miss Stott; I do not answer them. You provide the answers, under oath." Judge Schenck barely suppressed a smile.

"Now, if we may continue. You must keep a record on conduct. Every penal institution keeps a record on inmates. Miss Stott, I'd like to pursue another topic."

"Please do, by all means," Stott said, the sarcasm in her voice undisguised.

"Are you aware that some of the Samarcand residents are mentally undeveloped?"

"Yes, some are marginal mentally. There are different gradations."

"Are these girls segregated and treated differently from other girls?"

"We have to treat them differently."

Stott had taken the bait, and Nell moved in for the kill. "Do you mean they are put in Chamberlain and labeled troublemakers?"

Stott said sharply, "We do not label girls troublemakers, Miss Lewis. But yes, often girls who are mentally deficient get into trouble and are assigned to Chamberlain."

185

"Was Margaret Abernethy one of those girls?"

"Yes, Margaret has had a difficult time adjusting to Samarcand."

"Do you know the nature or extent to which this girl is handicapped?"

"I wouldn't choose the term handicapped. I know she is mentally undeveloped."

"Don't you know as a fact that she was committed to Samarcand at the request of her stepmother after her father subjected her to repeated incest from the age of ten, and he was sent to prison for that offense?"

A gasp went around the courtroom. Reporters took notes.

Don Phillips was on his feet before Nell finished speaking. "Objection by the State."

"Sustained," came an immediate, angry response from the judge. "Miss Lewis, unless you have proof of such facts and of such a prison sentence, I will not allow that question. You may ask the witness if she has seen the record of a conviction for incest."

"Thank you, Your Honor. Miss Stott, have you seen such records?"

"No, I have not."

"Do you otherwise know that Miss Abernethy was subjected to such violation by her male parent?" Nell wished she had been given sufficient time for trial preparation to allow her to obtain the father's criminal record.

"Objection, Your Honor," said Don Phillips.

"Sustained. The witness has testified she has not seen such a record of conviction. Please abandon this line of questioning, Miss Lewis."

"Yes, Your Honor. Miss Stott, would you say that some of these girls are unable to know the nature and seriousness of their acts and unable to know their rights?"

"I would say that some of them do not fully understand the gravity of their action. That's why punishment is administered. It is to teach a lesson and reinforce our rules."

Nell pushed on toward her objective. "When the staff gathered the suspects in a room in the Administration Building on the evening of March 12, 1931, were those mentally slow girls able to understand what you were doing?"

"I suppose so."

"You suppose? But are you certain?"

"No, I am not certain. We did not have the luxury of surety. There was no time for that indulgence. This was an emergency. We had a duty to ask questions to protect the others."

"Thank you, Miss Stott. I have no further questions."

Released from testifying, a shaken Estelle Stott stood and held onto the witness stand to steady herself, then slowly made her way to her seat behind the prosecution table.

The Testimony: Miss Crenshaw

"The State calls Miss Claire Crenshaw," Don Phillips announced.

Nell leaned toward George. "Where is MacNaughton?" she whispered. "Surely they'll call her?"

"They have to," George whispered back. "Or they almost have to. If they don't, it will be a sure signal something is wrong. I expect they will use her as the last of the Samarcand staff witnesses, try to get her to focus on the reform mission of the school, especially after your cross of Stott. My guess is she's up next." George and Nell stopped whispering and watched as Claire Crenshaw, wearing a no-nonsense gray tweed suit, passed the defense table as she marched to the witness stand to be sworn in.

"Miss Crenshaw," the solicitor began, "state your name for the record, give your employment, and state your address."

"I am Claire Crenshaw, supervisor of student government at Samarcand Manor. I reside in a staff apartment on the campus."

"Were you on that campus on the evening of March 12, 1931?"

"Yes. I was present at all times, as I usually am present at all times."

"Were you in the room when the staff rounded up the defendants the first time, and later when Sheriff McDonald and Deputy Mudd came to Samarcand?"

"Yes, on both occasions, first without the Sheriff and Deputy Mudd and later with them present. Miss Stott took notes, as did I."

"Who was doing the questioning?"

"Miss Ross, the Hall Matron, and Miss Stott were doing most of the questioning. Miss MacNaughton was also present."

"Do you have your notes with you today?"

"Yes, I have them." Miss Crenshaw held up a manila file she kept in her lap.

"Will you now refer to your notes and refresh your memory as to the statements and confessions of these girls?"

"Certainly." She reached into the file and removed a sheet of handwritten notes.

"Miss Crenshaw, please tell the Court what each of the defendants had to say."

"The following girls confessed to me to having set the buildings on fire: Josephine French, Delores Seawell, Margaret Pridgen , Estelle Wilson, Chloe Stillwell, Edna Clark, Bertha Hall, Virginia Hayes, Rosa Mull, Margaret Abernethy, Marian Mercer and Ollie Harding." She peered at her notes. "The others, Mary Lee Bronson, Wilma Owens, and Pearl Stiles, confessed to knowing about the fires. Well, actually, Pearl Stiles never admitted to anything. She was turned in by Hilda Godley and Ruth Craxy."

"It is your testimony that on the night of Thursday, March 12, 1931, you were present and heard fifteen of the girls say they took part in the burning?"

"Yes, I heard each one of them."

"Later on in the evening when Sheriff McDonald and Deputy Mudd came, did their statements change?"

"No, Sir, everything stayed the same. Pearl Stiles refused to admit to anything."

189

"Do you have more?"

"Well, yes. I would just like to say it was a very, very difficult and confusing time."

"Miss Crenshaw," Judge Schenck interjected, "do I understand you correctly that defendants Mary Lee Bronson, Wilma Owens, and Pearl Stiles did not admit to starting the fires, only knowing about them?"

"That's correct, Judge, but two other girls said Pearl admitted to taking part in the Bickett fire."

"Miss Lewis," the judge continued, "you may cross examine the witness."

"With your permission, Your Honor, my co-counsel, Mr. George McNeill, will conduct the cross examination."

"Please proceed, Mr. McNeill."

"On the evening of March 12, was there anyone present to represent the girls being questioned, and were they, in fact, in custody at that time?"

"Mr. McNeill," the witness interrupted, "it is my understanding that all of these girls are always in custody. But it is true that no one other than our staff members were at the first interrogation. The Sheriff and Deputy Mudd were at the second."

"You don't mean to say that the entire inmate population was in that one room, do you? They must have been singled out for a reason."

"Of course not. But I feel I am representing these girls all the time. I was very careful with them."

"Are you saying the atmosphere in that room was not the least bit intimidating on that night, that the girls were not frightened?"

"Mr. McNeill, it was our duty to protect all the girls at Samarcand. We had to get at the truth because of the danger to the rest."

"Miss Crenshaw, you testified that you are the supervisor of student government. Aren't you also in charge of discipline at Samarcand?"

"Yes, that is one of my duties."

"And it never occurred to you that, as the person in charge of discipline, your presence at and participation in this questioning just might have intimidated at least some of these girls?"

"No, it did not. It was never our intent to intimidate the girls, but to get at the truth."

"As a matter of fact, did you not tell them that night that arson was a capital crime?"

"I recall that Miss Stott said arson was a capital crime."

"She said this to each of the girls, or to the group?"

"It was, I believe, during her initial statement to the group."

"Do your notes show the individual statement of each separate defendant?"

"No, we did not question each defendant separately, we just let them talk, but all of the defendants agreed by remarks or gesture that they took part."

191

"One further question, Miss Crenshaw, were you, and are you, aware that many of these girls are at the lower gradations of mental development?"

"Yes, I have seen the records."

"Isn't there some doubt in your mind as to their ability to understand the gravity of charges against them?"

"Frankly, Mr. McNeill, that was not our concern at the time. We had a duty to investigate in order to separate the perpetrators from the rest of our girls. I do believe that all of the girls knew that burning the buildings was wrong."

"In other words, you saw as your duty not the protection of those suspected, but the protection of the other residents?"

"I wouldn't put it that way myself, but it's true our primary concern was to keep the rest safe. That's correct."

"Miss Crenshaw, I have no further questions." Before stepping from the witness box, Claire Crenshaw glowered at defense counsel and asked for consent to be excused, which the court granted. Don Phillips called Moore County Deputy Sheriff Larry Mudd to the stand.

"Oh my Lord," Nell whispered to George, "They aren't going to call her."

"Looks that way."

"I'll bet Agnes isn't up to it," Nell whispered back. "They're afraid she'll break under the strain, say something that will harm their case."

"You may be right. One thing for sure, everybody's going to wonder why she's not taking the stand, including the judge. Her absence can't hurt our case."

The Testimony: Deputy Mudd

Don Phillips stood as the deputy was sworn and approached the witness box.

"Deputy Mudd, were you on duty the night of Thursday, March 12, 1931?"

"Yes, Sir, I was," responded the deputy, a tall, thin man with a pleasant demeanor.

"Would you please tell the court what happened that night?"

"Around 8:30 or 9 P.M, Sheriff McDonald got a call from Superintendent MacNaughton. She said Samarcand was burning down and to please hurry. Sheriff McDonald asked me to go with him. It's about 20 miles from Carthage to Samarcand, so we arrived in about thirty minutes. When we got there, a heavy pall of smoke was covering the area. We beat the fire truck there, which arrived way too late to save anything. Miss MacNaughton, Miss Stott and Miss Crenshaw were out in front of the remains of Bickett Hall. Flames were too hot to go near Chamberlain. Almost all the girls were outside, milling about, highly excited, yelling."

Deputy Mudd coughed. "We met with the Superintendent and some of her staff, asked them what happened. They told us the fires had been set by the girls. Two fires at Chamberlain. One earlier that was extinguished, then the second fire I would place starting about 8 P.M.. Sheriff McDonald asked about suspects, and we were told they were already being held in a room in the Administration. With Miss MacNaughton, Miss Stott, and other staff, the girls were escorted into a room for questioning. We questioned each of the girls separately."

"Who was present besides the girls?"

"Miss MacNaughton, Miss Crenshaw, Miss Stott, and at least one hall matron."

"And who asked the questions?"

"CJ, I mean Sheriff McDonald, and me. I took notes as well. We questioned those girls until almost midnight and determined there was probable cause for arrest, but we had to arrest them without a warrant, owing to the time of night. Ten of the girls went to Troy, because we didn't have enough cells at that time. The other six we took to the Carthage jail."

"Did you determine that both Bickett and Chamberlain halls were dwelling buildings for the girls?"

"Absolutely. Some bedding had been pulled out of Chamberlain. Both it and Bickett were dwellings where people lived and slept."

"Thank you, Deputy Mudd," said the solicitor, turning to the defense attorneys. "You may cross examine."

Nell rose. "I'll be brief, Your Honor. Deputy Mudd, would you describe the defendants as excited and afraid while you were questioning them?"

"Miss Lewis, them girls were very tired by the time we got them together, but they were certainly still very excited. Afraid, that's a bit hard to say. But yes, I'd say they were afraid. They had already been singled out and questioned by the staff. And they had already been told the burning was a capital crime. A couple girls asked us what that meant, and Sheriff McDonald told them they could get the electric chair. I can tell you, it made

194

an impression. Them girls seemed to have the idea we'd just send them all home where they come from." He shook his head.

"One last question, Deputy Mudd. Did you gather, or did you see, any evidence that the fire had been started by artificial means, or that a volatile agent was added?"

"We looked, Miss Lewis, but fact is, if anything was used, it were gone up in smoke. We sent someone back out the next day to look for traces and found none. A frame building with a cedar shingle exterior don't need nothing like kerosene or gas. It's already like tinder with an accelerant."

"Your probable cause for arrest was based on statements of the defendants?"

"Yes, ma'm. That and some pretty strong circumstances. Like living in the dwelling, being in the area, and being an inmate on involuntary commitment, and, of course, the statements of the staff."

"That's all, Deputy, no further questions."

Deputy Mudd looked toward the defendants. "I want to say, them girls seemed to think we were just having a party or something. That's how young people are, don't understand life is serious business and what you do can bring other people to grief."

Don Phillips held up the palm of his hand to indicate to Deputy Mudd he should stop making extraneous remarks. "Your Honor," he said, "This completes our witness list, and the State rests at this time. The State would, however, like to enter a Nol Process, with leave, in the case of both Mary Lee Bronson and Wilma Owens."

"Well, there's a surprise," Nell whispered to George. "At least Phillips was paying attention to testimony that some of the girls only acknowledged knowing about the fires, not setting them."

"Please hand the Nol Process notices to the Clerk of the Court, Mr. Phillips," Judge Schenck said, pulling back the left sleeve of his robe to glance at his wrist watch. "Since this has been a rather long morning and we have a crowded courtroom, if the prosecution has no more witnesses I'm declaring this court in recess until two o'clock, at which time I expect the defense to present its case." As spectators began leaving the courtroom, Judge Schenck added, "Before rushing off to lunch, would counsel for both the prosecution and the defense meet with me briefly in my chambers?"

Nell turned to George, "If he had requested to meet with just us, or worse, just me, I would have expected to be raked over the judicial coals. Now I don't know what to expect."

"Neither do I," George replied. "But I am praying for something good."

6

The Trial: Defense

Don Phillips led the queue of four attorneys into Judge Schenck's chambers. The judge hung his robe on the brass hook of a coat tree near a window, moved slowly to his desk, took a seat behind it, and placed his hands beneath his chin to face the attorneys. "Please, sit down," he said, gesturing toward the leather chairs.

"Well," he said to no one in particular, "it seems we have a bit of a mess on our hands. And I've yet to hear the defense's case. Please allow me to make a few assumptions." He surveyed the attorneys. "I presume none of you objects?"

"No, your honor," they murmured in unison.

"First, I assume the State of North Carolina has no interest in executing sixteen teenage girls for capital arson. Correct, Walter?"

Walter Siler nodded assent. "I can assure you the Office of the State Attorney General has no such desire."

"Agreed, Your Honor," Don Phillips echoed.

"And the defense? You wish to present your case to the court?"

"We do, Your Honor." replied Nell Lewis.

"It also appears to me that the state's case has some weaknesses. Although, Nell, I am not impressed by your novel contention that the defendants should be excused because they

197

should never have been sent to Samarcand in the first place. But it is clear, Don, as your nol pros filings indicate, there is no testimony sufficient to convict some of the girls for being involved in starting the fires." Judge Schenck pressed together the fingers of both hands. "The entire initial interrogation and indictment process is hardly pristine, and I suspect we shall hear more about the mental capacity of some of the defendants." He exercised his fingers. "Is this correct, Nell?"

"Correct, Your Honor."

"On the other hand, testimony this morning leaves no doubt that some of these girls started the fires, and if the court is forced to find them guilty, it must also mete out punishment. So I would like to make a suggestion. Rather than having lunch, or while having lunch, why don't the four of you work out a plea the court can accept?"

Judge Schenck rose from his chair. "It is not outside the realm of possibility that such a plea might take the death penalty off the table, while insuring the defense the ability to make its case, provided sensationalism is kept to a minimum, and to plead for what it perceives as just sentencing." He glanced out the window. "These are, of course, merely hypothetical possibilities, as I shall not reach a decision until the case has been fully presented to the court." He extended his hand first to Nell and then to Don. "Now I wish the four of you an excellent and productive lunch break, and I hope to consult with you immediately prior to reconvening court."

"Yes, Your Honor," the quartette murmured as it filed out of the judges' chamber.

In the hall, Don Phillips asked, "Shall we gather in the jury room?"

198

"Sounds good to me," said George.

"Walter," said Don, "I'll send out for sandwiches and iced tea. The Attorney General's Office can pick up the tab. You folks have all the money in Raleigh."

"Always more than their share," Nell agreed.

"I'll buy," Walter conceded. "Now let's get to work."

Nell anticipated a prolonged session filled with hard bargaining, but once the food was delivered, they began to talk. Negotiations moved surprisingly quickly. "I'll open with an offer of guilty to second degree arson," said Walter. "We think that's fair. The state has no interest in convicting these girls of a capital crime, but these girls are guilty of an extremely destructive act, one that could have easily resulted in someone's death. They are not merely some misguided youth."

"That sounds like pretty high stakes, Walter," Nell responded. "What do you think George?"

"Well, some of these girls did intentionally set fires which burned down two state buildings, and we all know it," said George. "We're not going to get a dismissal of all charges. It's a reasonable offer, considering that first-degree arson charge carries the death penalty. But the offer ignores potential sentencing, and it ignores the fact that the girls bear varying degrees of culpability."

"The State has no problem with leaving sentencing to Judge Schenck," Don Phillips said.

"Nor do we," George replied. ""But the issue of varying degrees of culpability remains."

"So, how do you think it should be addressed?" Walter said. "We are willing to entertain a reasonable suggestion."

"Here are my thoughts," said Nell, re-entering the conversation. "Yes, it is true that some of the girls committed arson. But it is also true that what they endured at Samarcand drove them to do so. Under the circumstances, I think it reasonable to request that the State agree not to press for harsh sentences."

"The law provides for a sentence of four months to ten years for second degree arson, as you know," said Don. "I suspect the State's definition of harsh sentences differs somewhat from that of the defense. What's your counter-offer?"

"No more than a year, with probation," Nell responded without hesitation. "These girls have served more than enough time at Samarcand."

"Nell, you know the State can't accept that," Walter responded. "Be reasonable. This is a serious crime. I think the best the Attorney General's Office could live with would be a recommendation of five years. That provides the Judge with the opportunity to reduce the sentence, and, of course, to suspend any sentence given in individual cases, which addresses the issue of varying culpability George raised. I think that is the best the State can do."

Nell sipped on her iced tea as she considered, then looked at George, who nodded his assent. Finally she said, "Don is correct about the parameters. I do indeed believe five years to be a harsh sentence. But if it is a recommendation only, then it might be acceptable."

"And what other condition would make it acceptable?" asked Don.

"The defense be allowed to present its case and closing arguments," Nell replied. "That would allow us to address all of the issues George raised."

"What exactly does that mean, Nell?" asked Walter. "We're now down to fourteen defendants, and I, for one, do not wish to see all of them parade to the witness stand. That would transform this case into a trial of Samarcand."

"Perhaps Samarcand SHOULD be on trial. What happened to those girls at that godforsaken place certainly would be relevant to sentencing," Nell shot back. Noting Walter's displeasure, she took a breath and softened her response. "We don't want a circus. We just want to be allowed to make our case to the judge in open court."

"I think Nell's request is fair," George added. "Presenting our case in no way counters your agreed upon sentencing recommendation."

"Allow us to call two former Samarcand employees for the defense, to balance the prosecution testimony of Miss Stott and Miss Crenshaw," Nell continued. "And we want to call Dr. Crane, whom we all know and respect, to testify about the mental capacity of the four girls he examined. And, of course, we want to put some of the girls on the stand. There is no need to call them all." She ran her finger around the rim of her glass of tea. "Might we agree on up to six of the defendants, plus the ability to make closing arguments?"

"That sounds reasonable, so long as you remember to avoid the sensational, and to expect vigorous and immediate objections if you go off on a tangent," Phillips cautioned.

"That's acceptable, of course," George replied.

Nell agreed and added, "We'd like to request one other consideration. It won't affect the trial proceedings. We'd like the State to agree not to announce the plea deal in open court until after all testimony is completed."

"I don't see a problem with that," Walter said. "How about you, Don?"

"No, not at all."

"Then we have a deal?" George asked.

"Let's call break," Walter replied. "We can fortify ourselves with lunch and see how this plays out with Schenck."

The Afternoon Session

Promptly at two, Judge Schenck reconvened court without reference to the successful plea negotiations. He immediately called upon the defense to present its case, noting that George McNeill had deferred to Nell as the lead counsel.

"Wish me luck," Nell whispered to George.

Suddenly the enormous responsibility of her first trial hit her. She felt as if every eye in the packed courtroom focused upon her, all ears strained to catch her every word. This was not how she had envisioned her courtroom début, here in tiny Carthage, representing a pack of adolescent fire-starters. Seeking inspiration, she glanced up at the courtroom's

202

impressive high ceilings, the beauty of its chandeliers, and reminded herself this trial was not about her reputation, but about these girls who had been violated by the very institution she had once supported. They deserved the best she could now give them. She would play the cards she was dealt, and play them well.

"If it please the Court, "she said, "the defense calls Lottie Mitchem."

Silence settled over the courtroom as tiny Miss Mitchem, wearing a plain blue frock, took the stand.

"Please state your name and your relationship with Samarcand."

The woman straightened her back and looked at Nell. "My name is Lottie Mitchem. I was a teacher at Samarcand from August 1929 until July 1930."

"Please give us your general impression of conditions there."

"They were terrible. Windows without panes, girls forced to sleep on the floor in the cold, most of the beds and other furnishings broken, bedbugs, supplies difficult to obtain."

"Did you ever have occasion to observe the medical treatment the girls received, and did you find problems?"

"Yes, indeed I did."

"Please provide the court with specific examples."

"I hardly know where to start. Some of the standard practices defied common medical protocol. Girls with venereal disease were not isolated after treatment, but were housed in the general population, with the result that venereal disease was rampant." At the mention of venereal disease by this frail woman, a rumble swept the courtroom, but quickly subsided when Judge Schenck expressed disapproval.

"Outbreaks of scabies were treated in the same manner, with the same results. I was denied even the most basic implements for hygiene, like tooth brushes and tooth paste for the girls."

"Were medical staff ever ordered to refuse treatment of the girls? And if so, by whose orders?"

"On more than one occasion I heard Superintendent MacNaughton tell the nurse, Bessie Bishop, not to treat the girls. Burns obtained while cooking, for example, she was told not to treat and not to report. Miss MacNaughton forbade treatment of some girls with severe cases of poison oak, saying the girls deserved it for venturing where they should not have gone, and to let them suffer as a lesson to them."

"You yourself heard Miss MacNaughton forbid these treatments?"

"Yes, I was present in the hospital with the girls and Nurse Bishop. One girl who had been badly beaten, I sent her to the hospital for treatment, and Miss MacNaughton said no treatment could be applied. But when the Superintendent left, the nurse treated her anyway." Miss Mitchem gathered her courage and stated, "She also ordered me not to treat or report dog bites."

"Please explain to the Court why you received requests from the girls for the treatment of dog bites?" Nell said.

"The Superintendent has a large terrier, Jack, she treats him like a person. He bites the girls. Miss MacNaughton thinks more of him than of the poor dear girls, who are instructed to let him roam at will. I get the impression Miss MacNaughton rather enjoys seeing him nip at the girls."

Don Phillips was quickly on his feet. "Objection, Your Honor. This is an outrageous and completely unfounded supposition."

"Objection sustained," said Judge Schenck. "Miss Lewis, you are again approaching the sensational, which I warned you would not be tolerated."

"One more question on this issue, Judge, which I assure you will avoid supposition," said Nell.

"Proceed very carefully."

"Miss Mitchem, did you ever observe Miss MacNaughton compare the girls with her dog Jack?"

"Yes, I did. She gave a birthday party for Jack, which all the girls were forced to attend. At the party she told the girls they were low-down, from terrible homes, and asked them if they didn't wish they were as good as Jack."

A murmur ran through the courtroom. Judge Schenck knitted his brow and drummed his fingers on the judges' bench. "No further questions, Miss Mitchem," Nell said, as another low buzz swept the spectators.

"Miss Mitchem," Don Phillips addressed the witness as he gingerly moved forward. "I have only two questions for you. Both may be answered with a simple yes or no. First, is it true that you have no idea how frequently Miss MacNaughton attempted to obtain state funding, or for what amounts?"

"Yes, that is true."

205

"And second, did you ever personally witness a girl at Samarcand receive corporal punishment?"

"No, I did not."

"One more question, Miss Mitchem. According to your testimony, you were not still employed by Samarcand, and were not there on the night of the fires. Is that correct?"

"Yes, that is correct."

"In light of your response, may I ask whether you like Agnes MacNaughton?"

Miss Mitchem answered, "As I have testified, I disagreed with many of her practices."

"That is not what I asked, Miss Mitchem. I asked if it would be fair to say that you do not like Agnes MacNaughton. Just answer the question, please. A simple yes or no will do."

Miss Mitchem's voice was firm. "Yes and no. Yes, it is fair to say I did not like her, and no, I do not like her." At this, Judge Schenck's eyebrows lifted and Nell thought she saw him barely suppress a smile.

"I apologize, Miss Mitehem, but I do have just a few more questions. You testified that venereal disease was rampant at Samarcand. Is this correct?"

"Yes, that is correct."

"Then venereal disease must have been frequently treated?"

"Yes, it was."

"Do you know how often it was treated?"

"No, I do not. I was not the nurse."

"Well, Miss Mitchem," said Phillips, "I do. According to Samarcand's biennial reports, treatments for various forms of venereal disease averaged about six thousand per year. Would you say this figure indicates that the girls at Samarcand were rampantly promiscuous?"

Furious, Nell leapt to her feet. "Objection, Your Honor!"

"I remind you, Miss Lewis, that your witness raised the issue," said the judge. "I will allow the question, but, Mr. Phillips, it is your turn to tread softly."

Regarding the solicitor with contempt, Lottie Mitchem answered, carefully choosing her words, "That is your characterization, Mr. Phillips. I can only say that they are normal young women, and it was neither my professional duty nor my inclination to observe, record, or characterize their sexual behavior."

"I have no further questions of this witness, Your Honor. She may step down," said Mr. Phillips.

Emboldened, Nell called her second witness, Fronnie Harrell. "Miss Harrell, what was your association with Samarcand."

"I was a teacher there this year."

"You heard Miss Mitchem's testimony that girls with venereal disease were not separated from the general population. Can you please tell the Court whether you witnessed the same situation?"

"Yes, I did. Infected girls in my hall, although treated for venereal disease, were not separated from the general population. And I would agree with Miss Mitchem that the spread of venereal disease was a major problem at Samarcand. This disease may be spread through unhygienic practices, like sharing toilet facilities."

"Were beatings frequently administered to the girls?"

"Yes, they were."

"Please tell the court your understanding as to how these beatings were carried out."

"I was told by several residents they were forced to lie face down on the stairs, and while in this position, members of the staff held their arms and head while another staff member administered the beating."

"Did you see bruising that resulted from these beatings?"

"Yes, I did."

"No further questions, Your Honor."

Don Phillips quickly approached the witness. "Miss Harrell, did you ever actually see a Samarcand resident beaten?"

"No, I did not. Corporal punishment was administered in Chamberlain Hall by other staff members."

"Then you cannot honestly swear that the bruising you observed came from a beating, can you?"

"No, I cannot, although it was consistent with reports."

"And since you were not residing in Chamberlin Hall, you have no direct knowledge of the behavior of the girls assigned to it, is that correct?"

"Yes, that is correct, Mr. Phillips."

"There might have been, in fact, good reasons that corporal punishment was employed, especially for the girls in Chamberlain. Is that not so?"

"In my opinion, nothing justified the nature of the beatings those girls received."

"As a teacher, Miss Harrell, do you consider yourself an authority on discipline techniques, especially for girls who continue to behave badly and disobey rules?"

"I am not an authority on such matters," said Miss Harrell, "but I know what is humane, and I know these are not hardened criminals, but only young people in our care."

"Is it not true that you were recently discharged as an employee of Samarcand Manor?"

"Yes, that is true."

"Thank, you, Miss Harrell," said the prosecutor. "Your Honor, I have no further questions of this witness."

Phillips is good, thought Nell, he goes straight for the witness' weakness. But he would, she felt confident, have a tougher time with her next witness. "If it please the court, the defense calls Dr. Harry Crane." Her witness sworn, Nell began her questioning. "Dr. Crane, please state to the court your name, address, and occupation?"

"I am Harry W. Crane. I reside in Chapel Hill, North Carolina, where I am Professor of Psychology at the University of North Carolina. I am also Director of the State Bureau of Mental Health."

"What is your specialty?"

"I specialize in psychology, particularly in the treatment of mental diseases."

"Do you make evaluations of people as to their mental capacities?" asked Nell.

"Yes, in my work and practice, I have made hundreds of evaluations using interviews and standard tests."

"Your Honor," said Don Phillips, "the prosecution stipulates that Dr. Crane is an expert in the field."

"Thank you, Mr. Phillips," said Nell. "Dr. Crane, at my request did you examine some of the defendants in this case?"

"I examined four of the girls."

"Did you make notes of your evaluations of the girls?"

"I did, and I have those records with me."

"Please refer to your notes and tell the court the results of your examinations of each of the four defendants, specifically, what you determined to be the mental age of each?"

"Certainly." Dr. Crane read from the notebook in his left hand. "Margaret Abernethy, nine years and eight months. Margaret Pridgen, eight years and ten months. Pearl Stiles, nine years and nine months. Marian Mercer, eleven years and nine months."

"In your expert opinion, none of the four defendants you examined has the mental capacity of even a twelve-year-old?"

"That is correct."

The Samarcand defendants seated to the right of the witness stand glanced at each other, the two Margarets and Pearl frowning, Marian suppressing a giggle.

"One final question, Dr. Crane. In your opinion as an expert in the field, do any of these four defendants possess the mental capacity to determine right from wrong?"

"It is my professional opinion that they do not."

Several defendants rolled their eyes; others looked down at the floor. Pearl Stiles stared hard at Dr. Crane.

"Thank you. Your witness, Mr. Phillips."

"The prosecution has no questions for this witness."

Phillips' strategy of not cross-examining Dr. Crane caught Nell by surprise, but she recognized it as a shrewd move. Harry's expert opinions were just that, opinions the judge would give the weight he chose, and no matter what the solicitor asked, Harry's opinions would not change. As Dr. Crane left the witness stand and walked back to his seat, Nell quickly reviewed her notes on the six defendants she had decided to call. She had carefully considered the order in which she would call them, arranging their testimony to create the best possible impression and to make cross-examination the most difficult. She led with Edna Clark, at seventeen one of the oldest defendants, and well spoken. Nell watched courtroom eyes follow Edna, an attractive brunette, as she strode confidently to the witness stand to be sworn.

Nell advanced Edna through her personal information, separated parents, father a drunkard, no work history, placed in Samarcand "because I wouldn't go to school and went with boys" against her father's wishes, then quickly moved to Edna's experiences at the reform school.

"Did you like Samarcand, Edna?"

211

"No, they treated you terrible."

"Were you ever beaten?"

"Yes'm. Three times. Once so hard they had to send me to the hospital." Edna rubbed her shoulder.

"Did more than one teacher administer punishment?"

"Yes'm. Once five teachers did."

"Now, Edna, please tell us where you were when the fires broke out."

"I was locked in my room in Chamberlain. I was sick. I looked out and saw Bickett burning. I was in my room when both fires started in Chamberlain."

"We have heard testimony that you were involved with the Chamberlain fires. How do you explain that?"

"I did hear several girls say they were going to burn Chamberlain, especially Margaret Pridgen. I told Miss MacNaughton, and she asked me if I helped. I said yes, but I didn't help." Edna cast her eyes downward.

"Then why did you say you were involved?

"I wanted to get out of Samarcand. I thought if they believed I was a big troublemaker, they would send me home. I would have said anything to get out of there." She looked up at Judge Schenck.

"Thank you for your testimony. I have no further questions."

Don Phillips rose to ask a single question. "Miss Clark, so that everyone understands, on the night of the fires when you were questioned by the Samarcand staff, you told a fib, that you had helped set the fires. Is that correct?"

"Yessir. But I just said it hoping to get out." Phillips turned on his heel. "No further questions for this witness."

Josephine French next took the stand. A petite fifteen-year-old with light brown hair pulled straight back and held in place with a tortoise shell comb, she folded her hands in her lap and looked intently at Nell.

Nell quickly established biography, Josephine born in Concord, lived in textile town of Haw River in Alamance County when committed to Samarcand, mother a silk mill worker deserted by the father, Josephine herself a child worker in the hosiery mill. "Please tell the court why you were sent to Samarcand Manor," said Nell.

"I was never in any trouble, but to be honest, I did not like school too much. When I was fourteen, I did meet a boy, he was in the Navy. I liked him. He was older, kind of full of himself, but he was nice to me, told me how pretty I was. I never had a man say I was pretty." Josephine smoothed her hair. "Mama didn't approve of me seeing him because he was older than me, and he had a car. It was old, but it ran good. Mama got up with the welfare people who said they would look after me, but I don't think she had no idea what kind of place they sent me to."

"Were you ever beaten at Samarcand?"

"I was beat by Miss Crenshaw for sneaking a letter into my room and hiding it. We was not allowed to receive mail from anyone except on a list. We could not write to anyone except persons on a list. What we wrote was read before it went out.

213

We wasn't supposed to tell what was really going on at Samarcand."

Josephine looked at the judge. "May I have a sip of water, please sir? My throat's sort of scratchy," Judge Schenck nodded at the bailiff, who brought Josephine a tumbler, from which she took a swallow before she again apoke. "The next day after the letter was found, I was taken to a room where Miss Crenshaw was. I was stripped down to my underwear and a sheet over my back and I was laid face down on a rug. Miss Crenshaw brought in four girls to hold my arms and legs. Then she hit me about thirty times. The girls holding me was crying. They put witch-hazel on my back when they finished whipping me, and I was locked in a room without a bed, with only a blanket on the hard floor. They did give me some food which didn't taste very good. I was kept there several days."

"Did you ever attempt to escape from Samarcand Manor?"

"Oh yes, ma'am. About a month after they whipped me, I tried to escape. I was picked up in less than an hour by a guard and sent directly to Miss MacNaughton's office."

"One last question, Josephine. Did you ever confess to setting the fires at Bickett or Chamberlain?"

"No, ma'm, I did not. I never confessed to nothing, and anybody who says I did is a liar. I was locked up in confinement in one room when the fires broke out. The teachers told me I was being sent to jail for something else, they didn't say what. Sometimes I wish I had been burnt up in the damn fire." Don Phillips registered a half-hearted objection to Josephine French's final comment, which the judge sustained with a bemused sigh. Don declined to cross examine.

Dolores Seawell, a gangly fifteen-year-old from the coastal fishing village of Swansboro in northeastern North Carolina, followed Josephine French to the stand. She testified that her father died when she was a child, and her mother remarried and began a second family. When Dolores was thirteen, her mother and stepfather began to worry about her "running around," and she was committed to reform school because "a lady told my mother she thought Samarcand would be good for me."

"Did you like Samarcand?" Nell asked.

"I did at first, but not later on. It was awful. I ran away three times. They kept me in the discipline cottage most of the time I was there."

"Why were you assigned to the discipline cottage?"

"At first for being rude, then for running away."

"Were you beaten while at Samarcand?

"Yes, ma'm, once. Miss Crenshaw, she beat me with a leather strap with holes in it, beat me so bad it drew blisters."

"And on the night of the fire, did you confess to helping to burn either of the buildings?"

"No, ma'm, I did not. I was locked in my room in Chamberlain for running away when the fire started in Bickett, and I was in my room asleep when the fire started in Chamberlain. I told Miss Crenshaw I didn't know anything about the fires. Miss Crenshaw told me and two other girls we were going to jail for something else."

Nell next called Marian Mercer, knowing her testimony would be risky and her deafness would be a problem, but Nell was convinced that placing on the stand only defendants who

215

claimed innocence would be bad strategy. Marian seemed a good choice to admit involvement with the fires. Abandoned by her mother after her father drowned, most of her life she had depended upon the kindness of strangers who betrayed her trust.

Nell spoke slowly and clearly, drawing close to the witness stand. "Marian, please tell the court what you thought of Samarcand."

"I hated it," said Marian with her unique pronunciation of some syllables. "I'd rather be anywhere than Sama'cand."

Judge Schenck learned forward, cocking his right ear in Marian's direction. "Would the witness please speak more loudly," he instructed.

"Your Honor," explained Nell, "Miss Mercer has a handicap. She is deaf."

"Deaf!" exclaimed Judge Schenck. "How can she understand the questions? How can she testify?"

"I would ask you to excuse this witness," interjected Don Phillips.

"Your Honor, her testimony is important," said Nell. "We simply have to speak clearly and a bit more loudly, and allow her the time she needs to respond."

Judge Schenck looked at Marian with a sympathetic expression on his face. "Please proceed, Miss Mercer," he said, "as you are able."

Nell continued. "Were you beaten?"

"No, ma'm. I never was. They was just mean to us. Our rooms was full of bedbugs, cou'n't hardly sleep. In the winter it was cold, and they always made us work so hard, in the kitchen, in the laundry, in the fields, until our hands was bleeding. It was just always hard work. And I never knew how long I would have to stay. I been there more than two years, no end in sight."

"Did you confess to starting one of the Chamberlain fires?"

Marian watched Nell's lips when questions were asked. "Yes, I did. I told M' Stott that M'ret P'idgen and me used a stocking to set the first fire at Chamberlain Hall. But it didn't do hardly no damage. They put it out real quick."

"Why did you decide to start the fire?"

"I thought it would get me home, least ways out of Sama'cand."

Again the solicitor declined to cross-examine, appearing nonplussed by the deaf witness. Nell called Rosa Mull as her next-to-last witness. At thirteen the youngest of the defendants, Rosa's background, Nell believed, would evoke sympathy from the spectators and the judge. As soon as Rosa was sworn, Nell began a line of questions designed to do just that.

"Where is your home?"

"Before Samarcand, I lived in Rutherfordton."

"That's in the mountains, isn't it?"

Rosa nodded. "Yes, ma'm."

"You lived there with your mother and father?"

"Just with my father."

"Is your mother living?"

"Yes, ma'm."

"Where does she stay?"

"My mother Mary, she's at the State Hospital for the Insane up at Morganton."

"Do you know whether your mother suffers from any disease?"

"Yes, ma'm, She's got something they call pell-a-gra. I don't exactly know what that is, but it sounds terrible. I never noticed her being insane. I don't like that at all, people saying my mother is crazy." Rosa looked at Judge Schenck. "I love my mother."

"Your father, what does he do for a living?"

"He's a farmer. He works awful hard."

"Do you have brothers and sisters?"

"A sister and two brothers, all younger than me."

"Why were you sent to Samarcand, Rosa?"

"They said it was because I was running around. My daddy whupped me because I went off and didn't ask him. I run off to Marion and stayed with a boss man at a mill, tended his children for two weeks. He had a nice house, and he slipped me some money to buy myself things I needed, which my daddy couldn't pay for."

"Now, Rosa, I want you to answer this question honestly. Did you ever have sexual intercourse with men?" Nell heard whispers ripple though the crowd.

"Yes, ma'm, about four times, while I was at Marion. It wasn't my idea. I didn't hardly know what was happening, only I was supposed to do what he wanted." The whispers grew louder and Judge Schenck rapped his gravel to restore order. Rosa continued, "My daddy got me put in jail when I come home.

218

Then he had me sent to Samarcand. Nobody did nothing about the boss man."

"How old were you then, Rosa?"

"I was twelve years old."

"And did you like Samarcand?"

"No, ma'm. It was awful there. I ran away three times, but I always got caught and brung back. Ain't nowhere much to go way out there, really."

"And were you beaten?"

"Once."

"For running away?"

Rosa smiled. "For whistling out the window."

"For whistling out the window?"

"I got tired of being shut up inside. I just wanted to see how far I could make the sound go, and maybe somebody would whistle back at me."

"Would you please tell the Court where you were on the night of the fires at Samarcand?"

"When Bickett caught, I was locked in my room in Chamberlain. Then I was let out into the yard and I was on the steps the first time Chamberlain caught. The second time, I was in bed."

"Did you confess to Miss MacNaughton or any of the teachers that you helped start the fires, or you knew about them."

"No, ma'm, I never did. Miss MacNaughton never asked me nothing. Some of the other girls told her I had matches, and the next day the teachers found matches on me. I took them because if they found them, they would think I set the fire and send me home."

"That is all, Rosa, thank you, unless the Solicitor has some questions."

Don Phillips shook his head in the negative, and Rosa stepped down to rejoin the other defendants.

"The defense calls Margaret Abernethy."

Nell took a deep breath as she prepared to question the frail girl in the yellow print frock who made her way to the witness stand, took her seat, and brushed her blonde hair from her face. Nell had wrestled with her conscience about using as a witness this fifteen-year-old girl with the mentality of a nine-year-old child. But more than any of the other girls, Margaret Abernethy personified Nell's contention that many of the defendants should never have been placed at Samarcand, and Nell salved her conscience by assuming Margaret was unable to fully understand the significance of her testimony.

"Tell me about your mother, Peg."

"She's dead."

"What was her name?"

"I don't know." A gasp went up from the spectators, who realized fathers might frequently be anonymous, but assumed that mothers were always known to their children.

"Your father, do you know his name?"

"Ivey. Ivey Abernethy."

220

"And is he living."

"Yes, ma'm."

"Where does he live, Peg?

"Raleigh, up at Central Prison." Again the spectators gasped.

"Do you know why he is in Central Prison?"

"When he got drunk, he would lay up with me."

"You mean he would have sex with you, don't you, Peg."

"Yes, ma'm."

A loud murmur swept through the courtroom, and Nell thought she heard sobs. This time Judge Schenck brought down his gavel. "There will be order in the Court. Continue, Miss Lewis, but tread softly."

"Did this happen over a long period of time?"

"About three years, when my stepmother caught him."

Phillips was instantly on his feet. "I think Miss Lewis has established that the witness was abused by her father, and I see no need for further details."

"Sustained," responded the judge. "Please desist from soliciting further details about this matter, Miss Lewis."

"Yes, Your Honor. I believe the point has been made. Peg, was this the reason you were sent to Samarcand?"

"Yes, ma'm. My stepmother had me sent away because she said I was a bad girl and I got my father in trouble."

"Please tell the court how you felt about Samarcand."

221

"Worst place I ever was. Tried to escape twice."

"Were you beaten?"

"Four times, straps and switches. They cut off my hair when I tried to run away."

"Why do you suppose they cut off your hair?"

"To make me look ugly. Miz Stott said take away my crown of glory."

"Please tell the Court of your involvement with the fires at Samarcand."

"Some of us Chamberlain girls were in the dining room when Bickett caught fire. We started taking things out of the rooms in Chamberlain, and then some of us decided to set it on fire. I got some matches and Margaret Pridgen went in the attic and held a stocking while Marian Mercer lit it. The staff put it out quick, before it could do any damage. I thought if I set the building on fire, they would get rid of me. The second time Chamberlain caught, I was in bed and just saw the fire. I was surprised it got so big, but I did feel happy when I saw flames leaping up in the air."

"Did you tell Miss MacNaughton what you just told the Court?"

"Yes, ma'm, I did, because it was the truth."

"No further questions, Your Honor."

"The State has no questions of this witness, Your Honor," said Don Phillips.

With a greater sense of relief than she could ever have imagined, Nell said, "The defense rests." She felt sorry she had

222

to publicly expose such deeply private aspects of the girls' lives, especially with reporters taking notes which would appear in newspapers across the state. She consoled herself with the knowledge that records already existed concerning these matters, and concealing them now would not work to the defendants' advantage.

Don Phillips nodded at Nell before he addressed Judge Schenck. "If it please the Court, after meeting with defense counsel the State has agreed not to prosecute any of the defendants on the first count of the Bill of Indictment, first degree arson. The State has agreed to accept a plea of guilty on the second count of attempt to commit arson."

A jumble of reporters left their seats and stampeded for the doors, at which Judge Schenck pounded his gavel and shouted, "Order in the court." The reporters slowed their rush down to single file in quick time. Judge Schenck turned toward the defense table. "Miss Lewis, Mr. McNeill, for the record, do you concur this is a correct statement by the Solicitor?"

George McNeill replied, "Yes, Your Honor," to which Nell nodded her assent with a barely audible, "Yes."

Judge Schenck wasted not a moment before saying, "Very well. The Clerk will record the pleas of the defendants as the Court calls out their names alphabetically. Defendant Margaret Abernethy: Guilty as to the second count of the indictment, Defendant Edna Clark: Guilty as to the second count of the indictment....."

Nell barely heard the judge pronounce these words. She was acutely aware of the fourteen girls who sat only a few feet away. The courtroom was silent, not a whisper, not even a cough, as the judge continued to read. Nell retreated into her

223

own thoughts, turning to the closing arguments she must deliver. The girls' lives were no longer in jeopardy, but with a plea of guilty entered it was up to her to convince the judge they deserved no further punishment, that Samarcand had already punished them enough. From the depths of her soul she believed this. But she knew her personal feelings were immaterial to the Court; she would have to persuade Judge Schenck, who was saying, "All evidence having been concluded and the pleas of the several defendants having been tendered and accepted through their respective counsel, the closing statements of counsel will now be heard. Mr, Phillips, you had opening argument, and since we have pleas in this case, I assume you will waive closing. I further understand that Miss Lewis will make the sole closing argument for the defendants." Nell nodded in assent.

Don Phillips made his way to the dais and turned so he faced both Judge Schenck and the spectators. "If it please the Court, this trial has aroused in all attending—counsel for the defense, prosecution, and spectators—intense feelings of sympathy and empathy." He cleared his throat. "Testimony heard today establishes the fact that, without question, many of these defendants come from sad circumstances—broken homes, the loss of parents, and have mental and physical handicaps. But the State of North Carolina endeavored to extend its hand to them, and despite these hard times has clothed and fed them, granted them educational opportunities, even provided them with lessons from the Holy Scripture, as the Statute requires it to do. No one can fairly look at the State and say it did not try to improve the lives of these girls and give them a decent chance to become productive citizens."

Don paused for effect, gazed for a few moments at the girls, who stared at him impassively. Then he turned to face only the judge. "These defendants chose to bite the hand that fed and clothed them, housed them, and stood as their guardian in loco parentis. They deliberately and maliciously attempted to burn their very place of respite, destroying property worth thousands and thousands of dollars. They placed lives in jeopardy and deprived other girls, like themselves, of the opportunities they chose to squander. In addition, while incarcerated some of the defendants twice set fire to county property, showing their utter contempt for the law and the lives of others. I believe the Court would be fair in giving these defendants what they have shown they deserve, not less than five years in State's Prison, where they cannot set another fire."

After a moment, the judge said, "Miss Lewis, you may give your closing for the defendants."

Nell hoped that neither Judge Schenck nor the spectators, and especially not the girls, would observe the tremble sweeping through her body. She felt woefully inadequately prepared; there had been no time to work on a closing statement. For the past two hours she had focused solely on obtaining the most favorable testimony possible from her witnesses. She had hoped for an adjournment until the morning, time to prepare the words she would now have to speak extemporaneously, upon which the future of fourteen of the state's most unfortunate young women depended. Take a deep breath and go for it, she told herself, show what you're made of, as she positioned herself to face the judge and the courtroom.

"Your Honor, there were two indictments brought here today. One, the formal legal indictment brought by the Solicitor; the other less tangible but no less real, against society for the presence of these children in a criminal court room. These children, like all other children, are products of their

225

environment, heredity, and the pressure society has brought to bear on them. Some were born mentally defective, others come from broken homes where parents were handicapped, where the girls were severely abused in body and soul. They are the products of the subtle forces which have played on them since birth. It is not a case of black and white, but of many shades of grey.

"These children," Nell continued, pointing to the defendants who sat motionless, their gaze fixed upon her, "were wards of the state. The State declared they were not getting proper discipline at home and North Carolina undertook to stand in the place of parents it deemed inadequate. The State recognized them as deprived children, yet is now asking to punish them severely for being human beings who found further abuse and deprivation at the hands of the State.

"I am not saying they should not be punished, Your Honor." Nell turned slightly toward the judge. "But I am saying that half-grown girls in a civilized community should not be laid on a whipping carpet when flogging has been abolished on the State's chain gangs. These children were wards of the state when the crime was committed. They are young, with their eyes toward the future, and I believe the State should give them every possible chance. Your Honor, it is my heartfelt belief that if these girls stood before the divine tribunal, they would not be adjudged guilty. Thank you, Your Honor."

Judge Schenck spoke to a hushed courtroom as Nell joined George McNeill at the defense table. "Thank you, Miss Lewis. The Court will reserve its decision in this case until tomorrow morning, when it will reconvene at nine o'clock. This Court stands adjourned."

The judge's postponement caught everyone in the courtroom by surprise. For a moment, stunned silence prevailed. The reporters still present recovered first and began to make their way to the doorways at the back of the courtroom. The spectators began to file out gradually, some glancing backwards toward the girls, making comments about what they had seen and heard, creating an unintelligible buzz. Still seated, Nell turned to George and asked, "What do you make of this?"

"Don't know," he replied. "It's been a long day, lots of emotional testimony, reason enough for an adjournment."

"I'm encouraged," Nell said. "I hope this means Judge Schenck is going to think hard about what represents a just sentence for each of the girls. He has a daughter, you know."

"Not much to do now except wait and hope. I guess we'll find out tomorrow morning. Why don't you come home with me for dinner? My wife would be delighted to have you over. No reason to go back to your hotel alone."

"Thank you, George, that's very thoughtful of you, and much appreciated," said Nell. "But I feel like being to myself tonight."

"Don't spend all night second-guessing yourself and thinking about what you might have said. I don't see how you could have delivered a better closing, so let it go. It's up to Judge Schenck now."

Back in her room, Nell fell across the bed exhausted. She awoke nearly four hours later and walked to the Rainbow for country-style steak, mashed potatoes, green peas, and sweet tea. The dinner crowd had long since departed, so she was able to eat her meal in peace. No one spoke to her about the trial, for which

227

she was grateful. When she returned to her room, she was not sleepy in the least. She pulled out a bottle of sherry from her luggage, glad she had decided at the last minute to pack it. Pouring three fingers of the golden liquid into a water glass, she settled into the upholstered chair next to the telephone table. After two sips of sherry, she picked up the phone and asked the operator to call Kate Johnson's home number in Pennsylvania. She was gratified to hear her friend's voice on the second ring.

"Hello, Kate, this is Nell."

"I know your voice, even when it sounds tired. How did it go today?"

"Honestly, I've no idea. The State did offer to drop the capital charges in exchange for a plea of guilty to second degree arson, which we accepted. At least that took the death penalty off the table."

"Sounds to me like a big win. Wish I could have been there to observe battling Nell in action. What's the range of penalty for second degree arson?"

"Four months to ten years. The State recommended five years. No idea what the judge will do. He'll announce his decision tomorrow."

"Surely he won't give those misbegotten girls the full five years," said Kate.

"Despite my best efforts at closing, I'm sitting here reproaching myself for not doing a better job. I feel there was something I could have said, some circumstance I ignored, which might have influenced the judge to arrive at a lenient sentence."

"Don't beat yourself up, Nell. You've done all you can, gone way above the call of duty. You've certainly more than earned any remuneration you might receive."

Nell laughed at the mention of remuneration. "They don't deserve even a day in prison, Kate, not a one of them. And if they have to serve time, I'll feel like I let them down somehow. You know I will."

"You'll be inclined to nail yourself to a cross. But please don't. Get some rest. I'll cross my fingers for tomorrow."

Moments after speaking with Kate, Nell felt a sense of loneliness begin to creep into her soul, not an acute pain, just a nagging, dull throb, one she knew well. She briefly envied the warmth and support of a companion some married professional women enjoyed, and allowed herself a fleeting indulgence in self pity. She recalled her youthful relationship with Lenoir Chambers, the pleasure she took in his presence and in sharing experiences with him. But that was the past, an increasingly distant past, one she could not allow to become a fantasy, a place to escape the loneliness of the present. Being a single woman had its advantages, no husband to please, freedom to pursue her own interests on her own time, such as being in Carthage fighting for the lives of the girls from Samarcand. Hers was a good life. She reclined on the bed, propped herself up with a pillow, poured another glass of sherry which she sipped until a warm, sleepy feeling came over her, and slept until morning.

The Sentences

When she and George arrived the next day, the courtroom was packed and reverberating with anticipation. Reporters

229

stood at the back near the doors, ready to bolt for telephones the minute the judge pronounced sentences. At nine o'clock sharp, Judge Schenck emerged from his chamber and the Clerk announced Court was in session.

Judge Schenck began, "The Court has considered and heard all the evidence presented, all testimony of States' witnesses, all testimony of witnesses for the defense, including testimony of several defendants themselves. The Court gives to that evidence every reasonable intendment which the law logically allows to follow. The Ccourt also has heard and considered the arguments of counsel, both for the prosecution and for the defense. Upon the pleas of the defendants given through their counsel, the Court finds as a fact and concludes as a matter of law, that each and all of the twelve defendants are, in fact, guilty."

He paused for a moment to allow a brief response from the crowd and the girls, then motioned for quiet. "Before entering sentence," he continued, "I will speak to the defendants." He looked directly at the girls, who sat barely moving, as if frozen in place. "You were initially, and justifiably, charged with a capital crime, and could have been tried for your lives and sent to the electric chair. The State did not wish to send you to the electric chair, and agreed to accept a plea for a lesser offense, for which you could be sent to the penitentiary for ten years.

"I do not want to do that, although I believe each of you understands what you did was wrong and you could be severely punished for it. You have said you would rather go to jail than be in Samarcand. You are going to have your choice. The length of your stay in the penitentiary depends entirely upon you. If you want to stay there for the full term of the sentence, just go down there and set something on fire. But under the sentence I am about to impose, if you choose to behave yourself, you can be released in little more than a year. Remember, the State is strong enough to hold you. It is my hope you will choose wisely."

His gaze still upon the defendants, Judge Schenck formally delivered his sentence. "In State vs. Josephine French, Virginia Hayes, Marian Mercer, Margaret Abernethy, Delores Seawell, Thelma Council, Ollie Harding, Bertha Hall, Chloe Stillwell, Estell Wilson, Edna Clark and Pearl Stiles, the judgment of the court is that these defendants and each of them shall be imprisoned in the State's prison for a term of not less than eighteen months, not more than five years. In the case of Rosa Mull, defendant shall be imprisoned not less than eighteen months, not more than five years, in the State's prison, judgment suspended upon condition she remain in good behavior. In the case of Margaret Pridgen, defendant is sentenced to State's Prison for not less than twelve months and not more than three years, judgment suspended upon defendant remaining in good behavior. This Court stands adjourned."

The courtroom exploded. Nell heard the defendants begin to cry, some with a high-pitched, almost keening sound, others with great, gasping sobs. She found the lighter sentence for Margaret Pridgen to be curious, since she had admitted to leadership in the setting of fires. Perhaps this disparity was because Margaret had caring family members who reached out to help her and would be available to take her back, now regretting having sent her away. The other girls weren't so lucky. Pearl Stiles sat rigid, defiant, perhaps recalling her proclamation, "Give me liberty or give me death."

Reporters and photographers rushed for the exits, pushing to be first out the door. Spectators, some crying softly, began a slow march out of the courtroom. Nell glimpsed three additional sheriff's deputies come over to help remove the defendants. As the girls stood, Margaret Abernethy in her yellow print frock, head down and crying, caught Nell's eye. Off to State Prison to serve time with Daddy, came into Nell's mind, and she struggled to suppress the thought.

"Well, it's over," she heard George say.

Nell gathered her notes and placed them in her brief case, and crossed over to speak briefly with Don Phillips and Walter Siler, before she spoke to George. "Yes, it's over for you and me. But not for the girls. Thank you for all your help. I deeply appreciate it and I certainly needed it. Now it's time I wend my way home to Raleigh."

"With all the attention the papers gave the trial, all the revelations about Samarcand, I expect there will at least be an investigation," George said, trying to remain positive.

"Yes, George, there probably will be," Nell agreed. "But in the end it won't much matter. The board of directors will back MacNaughton, the State Board of Charities will back the board of directors, and the State will back the Board of Charities. They'll brand the girls liars, abuses will be swept under the rug, and all will be forgiven. They may make a few changes, stop the beatings, change some medical practices. That's about the best we can hope for, but at least we fought the good fight."

She shook his hand and turned to make her way through the crowd into the courthouse lobby, ignoring reporters' calls for interviews. In the excited chatter around her, Nell heard snatches of opinions about the verdict: Them girls already been punished twice over for everything they did.....Looks like what they need is help, not punishment.......They haven't had a chance for anything since they've been born....More sinned against than sinning.......I'd have locked them up for the full ten years....No hope for any of them, might as well be put away for life.

Out of the corner of her eye, she glimpsed Beth Thompson interviewing Mrs. J. R. Page, Secretary of Samarcand's board of directors, a woman Nell had known and worked with for years. She paused, hoping to overhear the remarks, but Beth was wrapping up the interview. Nell heard Mrs. Page say confidently, "Only three girls had been whipped, and this was not done unmercifully. I am sure all the defendants who testified greatly exaggerated conditions at Samarcand."

Nell wanted to shout Liar! at the woman, but instead she moved slowly with the crowd toward the doors, glad to leave Mrs. Page behind. She reviewed the fate of the Samarcand girls. They had avoided capital punishment. Charges against two had been dismissed. Another two had received suspended sentences and avoided prison. The twelve sentenced to prison could be released in only a year and a half, less time than most would have continued to spend at Samarcand. Perhaps most significantly, the trial had revealed to the public the conditions and cruelties of the State's version of youth reform. She could, she told herself, have experienced a far less successful courtroom debut. Why, then, did she feel so defeated?

She kept walking, pushing through the crowd, through the courthouse doors, out into the sunshine. Briefly blinded by the bright light, she recovered her vision just in time to glimpse the wayward girls of Samarcand through the windows of a bus already headed for Raleigh and Central Prison. She shaded her eyes against the glare and watched the bus round the corner and disappear from sight.

The Epilog

Canadian Scotswoman Agnes B. MacNaughton and Southern aristocrat Nell B. Lewis, professional colleagues who found themselves on opposite sides during the Samarcand arson case, soon shared a common fate after the trial reached its conclusion. The superintendent of Samarcand Manor Reform School for Girls and the defense attorney for the Samarcand Sixteen both experienced depression with psychological breakdowns severe enough for hospitalization. Miss MacNaughton and Miss Lewis remained spinsters throughout their lives, leaving no progeny to mourn their passing. Agnes MacNaughton became a residential patient at Pine Bluff Sanatorium in Moore County, where she died in 1938. In 1940 a garden at Samarcand was dedicated in her name.

In June 1931 at Johns Hopkins Hospital in Baltimore, Nell Lewis had her adenoids removed and surgery on her jaw for infected bone. She also undertook a regimen of ovarian extracts prescribed to counteract effects of the abdominal surgery termed "appendectomy" she had undergone in 1930. In July and August, she received injections from Dr. Hubert Haywood of Raleigh for trench mouth. Dr. Haywood advised her not to live alone. In October she had a dentist remove her upper teeth, and she rented a room in her home to a young woman. She also began to attend Sunday School at Raleigh's Episcopal Church of the Good Shepherd. In December 1931, Lewis entered Tucker

Sanatorium in Richmond, Virginia, then briefly Watts Hospital in Durham, North Carolina, followed by admission to Broadoaks Sanatorium in Morganton, North Carolina. Her brothers sold her stocks to pay for her medical treatments, and she found herself in "dire straits" financially. In 1932 she entered psychoanalysis with Freudian analyst Reverend Elwood Worcester in Boston. During hourly sessions four times each week, she recalled repressed childhood experiences, especially her difficult relationship with her stepmother, Annie Blackwell Lewis. In 1934 she asked to become a patient at a Christian Science sanatorium. In 1936, her drinking required medical treatment. In 1937, Nell once again was employed by St. Mary's School to teach English, history, and Bible, until 1944 when she experienced another depressive episode, but resumed her teaching in 1954.

The crusader for the abolition of capital punishment, penal reform, and humane treatment of mill workers became increasingly more conservative following World War II. She verbally attacked many of her old friends, including the former president of the University of North Carolina, Frank Porter Graham, who as a fellow progressive had supported her campaign for the legislature in 1928. She also raged against Communism and school integration. She wrote of her political about-face, "After forty-two years I have discovered that a good deal of nonsense not infrequently masquerades as 'liberalism.'"

Nell continued her column "Incidentally" for the *News and Observer* until Tuesday morning, November 27, 1956, when her body was discovered in the front yard of her Raleigh home. At the age of sixty-three she had collapsed from a heart attack as she stepped out of her parked car the night before, holding her keys and purse in one hand. Four years later, the love of her life, former fiancé Lenoir Chambers, was awarded a Pulitzer Prize as editor of the Norfolk *Virginian Pilot,* for distinguished writing on school integration. He outlived Lewis by fourteen years, dying of a stroke on January 10, 1970, in his seventy-ninth year.

Defense attorney Lewis had made a post-trial visit to the twelve female defendants incarcerated at Raleigh's grim Central Prison in fireproof cells directly above death row, but her illness prevented her from maintaining contact with any of her former clients. Two decades later she wrote in her column, "I know the fate of only one of the sixteen, one of the four who got off. She killed herself. Hurrah for North Carolina!" Her reference was to Wilma Owens, the motherless girl who had been raped by a married man when she was eleven years old, and committed suicide two years after the arson trial, following in the footsteps of her father, who had died by his own hand in Wilma's presence in 1928. In 1929, prior to the Samarcand fires, Owens had been subjected to an officially-authorized "operation," likely sterilization recorded as appendectomy, and was recommended by Haywood County's W. G. Byers for nurses' training because she did "so well" as a patient helping nurses in the wards. However, in the aftermath of the arson trial, though nol prossed with leave, Wilma found her life so intolerable she ended it by drinking Lysol.

Margaret Pridgen, rightly or wrongly identified as the primary instigator of the Samarcand fires, whose family intervened on her behalf and helped achieve a sentence of three-to-five years probation on condition of good behavior, died of renal failure at the age of sixty-three on August 19, 1979, at Oak Manor Nursing Home in Kinston. Although there is no record of Margaret's being a victim of eugenics, it is probable that she, too, had been sterilized at some point in her life. Born of a fertile

236

mother who birthed eight children, and brought up in the Church of the First Born, also known as the Old Apostolic Lutheran Church, which believed childbearing to be a woman's primary value, Margaret was for a time married to a man named Jack "Chubby" Gurganious,. However, she never bore a child following her incarceration at Samarcand. In 1940, when she was twenty-four years old, while living with her parents on Dock Street, Margaret worked as a custodial attendant of the ladies' public restroom in downtown Wilmington.

Her nephew David Pridgen, now in his fifties, served as a casket bearer at her burial in Wilmington's Oakdale Cemetery. He remembers his Aunt Margaret as a gentle person who rocked him to sleep when he was a child. According to David, the Pridgens "drew a curtain around her life as it touched upon their lives." Margaret's youngest sister, whom she had cherished as a newborn in the month before Margaret was committed to Samarcand by her father Strange Pridgen, recalls that she was five years old the first time she saw Margaret:

> I was glad I had another sister, and I was excited to meet her. I heard about her. I used to ask my parents, 'Why is she not here with us?', and they said when I was a baby she would take all my brothers and sisters to the park without permission, so they decided she needed to be put in this school so they could tend to the rest of us. When I got older, I went to stay with her and her husband who was a truck driver. She was about eighteen years old when she married him, and I saw him abuse her so bad. She left him and came back to our parents in Wilmington, and her husband came after her, and my father told him not to come by any more. Margaret wanted a child so bad, but she couldn't seem to get pregnant. One time she bought some baby clothes in the hope she would have a child of her own. She loved my five children, so I told her I had children for her, too.

237

On December 3, 1959, Margaret was admitted to Dorothea Dix Hospital in Raleigh with a diagnosis of bipolar disorder because she again felt, as she termed her rebelliousness, "mean." She was discharged eighteen months later, on July 31, 1961. David observes that after her institutionalization at Dix, his Aunt Margaret became docile, in the manner of people who have been lobotomized.

Little is known about the fate of the other members of the Samarcand Sixteen. Pearl Stiles, author of the impassioned petition to Governor O. Max Gardner in the form of a letter from Moore County jail after the fires, in which she quoted Patrick Henry's famous "give me Liberty or give me Death," never received the courtesy of a reply from the governor. She was sentenced to eighteen months to five years in state prison.

Rosa Mull, barely thirteen at the time of trial, whose mother suffered from the nutritional deficiency disease pellagra, which causes dementia, received prayer for judgment for five years, contingent on good behavior. However, within three months, in September 1931, Rosa began serving a two-year term in state prison, instigated by her Rutherfordton community which expressed "dread of her influence" and wished her to be sent away. No official reason was given for "dread" of a girl so young, other than her habit of keeping late hours and not wishing to live with her father in a motherless home.

Marian Mercer, the deaf orphan who was the daughter of a drowned sailor and a deceased mother, ceased to be in the public eye.

Virginia Hayes was operated on for "appendicitis" at Moore County Hospital while incarcerated at Carthage jail, likely another sterilization performed without informing the patient about the type of procedure, arranged for the time between institutional release and return home, with no official documentation of the actual procedure.

Ollie Harding, orphaned by a mother who died of cancer and a father who was a paralytic unemployed "drunkard," ceased to be in the public eye.

Bertha Hall, whose father died of tuberculosis when she was a year old, and whose mother died of cancer, ceased to be in the public eye.

Josephine French, whose father abandoned her family when Josephine was two years old, and whose mother worked in a silk mill, ceased to be in the public eye.

Attractive, sociable Thelma Council also was operated on for "appendicitis" while jailed at Lumberton. She, too, ceased to be in the public eye.

Mary Lee Bronson, a tall, slender, attractive blonde who was well-mannered, ceased to be in the public eye.

Margaret Abernethy, whose father was an alcoholic plumber serving two years in the state penitentiary for forcing incest several times a week upon young Margaret, ceased to be in the public eye.

Research for *The Wayward Girls of Samarcand* failed to discover any of the sixteen defendants still alive, as the youngest would now be ninety-three years old, and the poverty of the girls' lives did not bode well for longevity. In the interest of inadequate storage space, Moore County burned all records from the Samarcand trial other than the official, handwritten sentences. The only remaining reports of the trial are newspaper articles and eyewitness accounts. Attorney George McNeill was awarded a $150 fee because the case was a capital felony. Dr. Harry Crane received $25 for his testimony.

In the wake of the fires and before the trial, Roy Eugene Brown, North Carolina's assistant commissioner of the State Department of Welfare, initiated an official study of conditions at the reform school. His recommendations effectively confirmed the allegations Nell Battle Lewis put forward in her defense of the girls, and on May 26, 1931, Samarcand's board of directors approved all his recommendations, including banning corporal punishment. On May 16, 1933, a letter from Moore County Hospital was sent to Samarcand patron Leonard Tufts, stating:

..For more than a year it has been evident to me that Miss MacNaughton was failing physically and mentally. On more than one occasion I have mentioned this to different members of the Board.... Nothing was ever done. Recently there have come to my attention most alarming reports of the management at Samarcand.... It is hard to get anywhere with Dr. Carroll and Mrs. Page. They are so prejudiced in favor of Miss MacNaughton. I am writing Dr. Carroll again requesting an investigation. If this does not get results, I shall bring the matter to the attention of the Governor, however much I should dislike to do so.

When North Carolina Public Welfare Director Roy Brown inspected the facility in 1934, he was not pleased with the slow rate of change, and declared, "The institution needs to be thoroughly reorganized with a person of ability and experience at the head." Shortly thereafter, Agnes MacNaughton departed from Samarcand on a six-month leave of absence because of "ill health," never to return. A 1940 account of the disciplinary ward described "mattresses on the floor with no beds, and a single washbasin and toilet for thirty girls." In her newspaper column in 1945, Nell Battle Lewis wrote that she wondered why the girls "hadn't burned the whole place to the ground," but acknowledged that "a general cleanup of administration" resulted in Samarcand being "at present a very well-run institution."

In the 1970s, Samarcand was briefly co-educational. In 2002, under Governor Mike Easley's recommended budget, male juveniles who had again been housed at Samarcand were relocated to other youth development facilities, leaving fifty-nine females. In 2008, North Carolina's Department of Juvenile Justice and Delinquency Prevention collaborated in a study of juvenile facilities regarding sexual misconduct by staff, abuse, and neglect. Samarcand manager Roger Reynolds, who has been employed at the facility since 1981, states that all allegations made at the all-female campus were thoroughly investigated, and the girls found to be safe and not being victimized. An effort was initiated by the North Carolina legislature in 2009 to close Samarcand because of budget constraints, but Samarcand remained open, with a capacity of 165 students.

The campus roads now have been asphalted and three buildings refurbished, including two computer labs. An October 7, 2009, editorial in the Southern Pines *Pilot* was titled "Samarkand Shows It Is Worth Keeping," and said of the girls, "...almost without exception they come from a background of deprivation, homes lacking in discipline and understanding, even love. For many students, the Samarkand experience represents their first exposure to caring adults who devote time and attention to individual needs." In April 2010, Governor Beverly Perdue proposed a $3,521,954 appropriation for Samarcand, and the last female residents were transferred to Swannanoa Valley Youth Development Center in Buncombe County. For the first time in its history, Samarcand housed an all-male juvenile offender population, coming full circle back to serving as an all-boys school, as when Dr. Hanford Henderson's private Marienfeld Open-Air School for Boys existed on that site.

In December 2002, Governor Michael Easley formally apologized for the eugenics program in effect from 1929 to 1974 which resulted in more than 7,600 sterilizations, including children as young as ten, often without prior authorization, justifying the surgeries with boiler-plate diagnoses of feeble-mindedness, sexual promiscuity, epilepsy, and poverty. More than 300 of these sterilizations had been performed upon Samarcand residents. In 2009, state lawmakers recommended that reparations be given to victims of this program, and a North Carolina historical marker was dedicated to the victims. A one-time payment of $50,000 has been suggested for living victims, but has yet to be paid, though North Carolina is the first state in America to approve such damages.

In North Carolina, arson in the first degree, burning an occupied dwelling, is no longer a death penalty crime, but is a Class D felony punishable by 38-58 months in prison for a first-time conviction. In 2010, a de facto moratorium on the death penalty is in place, following a decision by North Carolina's medical board that physicians cannot participate in executions, a requirement under state and federal law.

Samarcand Manor, opened in 1918 as North Carolina's State Home and Industrial School for Girls, has undergone several investigations and reincarnations. In 1973 two helicopters carrying state officials in the administration of Republican Governor James Holshouser descended on Samarcand. The raid, prompted by "complaints," forced the early retirement of Superintendent Reva Mitchell, who had

242

become assistant to Agnes MacNaughton in 1932 and superintendent upon MacNaughton's retirement, with forty-one years of service. The principal of Samarcand Manor School, Ralph Foushee, resigned when ordered to report to another training school at Swannanoa. In 1968 the official pamphlet for the celebration of Samarcand's 50th Anniversary referred to the 1931 fires with the brief statement, "Two dormitories, Bickett and Chamberlain, burned in the early nineteen thirties and were replaced by the new Bickett and Gardner." In 1974 Samarcand Manor was transferred from the Department of Corrections to the Department of Human Services. The original 224 acres of sand and clay terrain at the foothills of the Uwharrie mountains has grown to 460 acres of pine forest and rich farmland.

The founders of Samarcand meant well in the cultural context of their time, motivated by the desire to provide a haven for underprivileged girls on the brink of destruction, and to protect society from the consequences of illegitimate births and the ravages of venereal disease. Had the rights of those institutionalized at the reform school been respected through due process of law, and had Samarcand lived up to its stated promise rather than adding insult to injury with extreme physical, verbal, and emotional abuse, the arson of 1931 likely never would have occurred. Rather than choosing to set fire to the buildings because incorrigibility was understood to be the shortcut to discharge, the sixteen girls might have benefitted from residence at Samarcand and gone on to happier lives.

Most North Carolinians remain unaware of Samarcand's existence in the pine forest near the luxury golf resort of Pinehurst founded by James Walker Tufts in the sandhills. In 1943 Superior Court Judge Frank M. Armstrong stated to the grand jury conducting a mandated semi-annual investigation of this state institution:

> I have lived almost within the shadow of Samarcand ever since it was built, but it has always been sort of a place of mystery to me...I am inclined to believe that very little is known about the institution by the people and courts of the State, and I feel that this condition should not exist, especially by those of us whose duty it is to sentence a woman or a girl to an institution and not know nor care what becomes of her. Once the gates are closed behind her, she has very little opportunity to speak for herself, and there are few to speak for her.

In 2011, the State of North Carolina closed Samarcand.

On May 20, 2009, a posthumous Petition for Pardon of the Samarcand defendants had been presented to North Carolina's first female Governor Beverly Perdue, and still awaits her official attention. In 2012 Governor Perdue announced she will not seek reelection.

Notes on Sources

Surprisingly, there is no book-length treatment of the Samarcand arson of 1931 and the trial which resulted from it. *The Wayward Girls of Samarcand* is based on the sources discussed below, although this essay is not intended as a complete bibliography.

The narrative of the book relies heavily on primary sources. By far the most significant are the personal papers of Nell Battle Lewis, housed in two separate collections. The Lewis papers housed at St. Mary's School in Raleigh, which is the secondary school Lewis attended and where she later taught, contain material relative to her student days. The more significant collection for this book is housed at the North Carolina State Archives in Raleigh and contains Lewis's correspondence about and extensive notes on the Samarcand case. The transcript of the trial, ironically, was destroyed in a courthouse fire and no extant copy exists. However, a few documents relating to the case, including subpoenas for witnesses and the court docket, can be found at the Moore County Court House in Carthage.

Accounts of the fires at Samarcand, the jail-house fires in both Lumberton and Carthage, and the trial are taken from several newspapers, especially the *News and Observer* of Raleigh, Lumberton's *The Robesonian*, the *Morning Star* of Wilmington, the *Charlotte Observer*, The *Greensboro News*, the *Moore County News*, and the *Fayetteville Observer*. Material on the operation of Samarcand comes primarily from Samarcand's June 30, 1930-1932 Biennial Report; and its pamphlet 1918-1968, 50th Anniversary, Samarcand Manor, both of which can be found at the North Carolina Collection in the University of North Carolina's Wilson Library. Much of the material on Margaret Pridgen, the girl most responsible for the Samarcand fires, comes from interviews conducted by one of our authors, Anne Russell, with members of Pridgen's family in Wilmington.

Secondary accounts of the Samarcand arson and trial are found in a number of academic journal articles, which focus not on the events themselves, but upon various interpretations of their significance. Among them are John Wertheimer and Brian Luskey's "Escape of the Match Strikers: Disorderly North Carolina Women, the Legal System, and the Samarcand Arson Case of 1931," *North Carolina Historical Review*, Vol. 75, No. 4, October, 1988; Susan Cahn's "Spirited Youth or Fiends Incarnate," *Journal of Women's History*, Vo. 9, 1998; and "Imperial Modernity, National Identity and Capital Punishment in the Samarcand Arson case, 1931," *Nations and Nationalism*, Vol. 13, Issue 3, 2007, by Annette Louise Bickford. Susan Pearson's honors essay at the University of North Carolina, 1989, entitled "Samarcand, Nell Battle Lewis, and the 1931 Arson Trial," is especially useful for information about the establishment of Samarcand. The best study of Nell Lewis is Alexander S. Leidholdt's *Battling Nell, The Life of Southern Journalist Cornelia Battle Lewis, 1893-1956*. Baton Rouge: Louisiana State University Press, 2009.

Acknowledgments

The authors could not have written the story of the
Samarcand arson trial without the aforementioned scholars who
published their own research. We also are grateful to
Samarcand's manager Roger Reynolds, who took us on a tour of
the grounds and apprised us of the current status of the
institution. The Given Memorial Library in the Village of
Pinehurst generously provided us with a consultation room and
access to the Tufts Archives. David Pridgen of Wilmington,
North Carolina, shared his extensive private family archives so
we might better understand the circumstances of his aunt
Margaret Pridgen. Emily Wilson and Nan Graham served as
readers for the manuscript. Attorneys Stephen Culbreth and
Barry T. Winston advised on legal references. Former Wake
County legislator and attorney Howard Twiggs provided insight
into his professional experience with Samarcand beginning in
1959.

Author Anne Russell, mother of four daughters,
established an interest in Samarcand out of her activism on
behalf of women's issues, and her relationship in 1959 with a
"delinquent" adolescent sent to Samarcand for riding with a boy
in a car not his own. Melton McLaurin, father of three
daughters, continued his exploration of Southern history by co-
authoring the Samarcand story. Together we present a portrait
of North Carolina's Industrial and Training School for Girls at a
particular moment in time when an extraordinary event exposed

247

it to the public eye, in light of current events relating to the Samarcand story. Should anyone have information about the later lives of the Samarcand Sixteen, please contact the authors.

CPSIA information can be obtained at www.ICGtesting.com
Printed in the USA
BVOW04s1130271013

334774BV00008B/87/P